The Towering Wave

from the author of

The Individual and the Group (London: Allen & Unwin, 1939)
The Real and the Negative (London: Allen & Unwin, 1940)
Gandhi: A Prophecy (Oxford: Hall, 1948)
Related Multiplicity (Oxford: Hall, 1952)

The Towering Wave

B.K. Mallik

DK PRINTWORLD
Publishers of Indian Traditions

Cataloging in Publication Data — DK
[Courtesy: D.K. Agencies (P) Ltd. <docinfo@dkagencies.com>]

Mallik, Basanta Kumar, 1879-1958.
The towering wave / B.K. Mallik.
p. cm.
Reprint.
ISBN 13: 9788124607534

1. Peace. I. Title.

DDC 327.172 23

ISBN 13: 978-81-246-0753-4

First published in June 1953
by Vincent Stuart Publishers Ltd., London

First reprinted in India with fresh typeset in 2014

Printed and published by:
D.K. Printworld (P) Ltd.
Regd. Office: Vedaśrī, F-395, Sudarshan Park
(Metro Station: Ramesh Nagar), New Delhi – 110 015
Phones: (011) 2545 3975, 2546 6019; *Fax*: (011) 2546 5926
e-mail: indology@dkprintworld.com
Website: www.dkprintworld.com

To
Sadhu Baba

Foreword

It is an honour to be associated with the republication of philosopher Basanta Kumar Mallik's work. Born in 1879 and hailing from an old Meherpore (Nadia) family his academic and working career spanned Bengal, Nepal and Oxford in the first half of the twentieth century. His sojourn in England during both world wars considerably contributed to his meditations on conflict and peace. Although his strictly philosophical oeuvre consists of four major volumes on metaphysics, *The Towering Wave*, published in 1953, is written for a wider audience, packaging in literary form his seed ideas on conflict, history, society and prospects for a stable peace.

One can only describe the literary device he uses in this book as allegory, though he himself always rejected the term. His language is full of images, his poetic prose generously sprinkled with "quotable quotes" (e.g. "Life after all is meeting if anything"; "A city is not the heart of the state but only a 'process' or 'movement'" or "since theory and practice are essential to one another and appear and disappear together, it follows that a soldier, as such, no more fights than a theory, as such does"). He conveys his message through symbols, tantalizing suggestions and veiled references to current events interspersed with recognizable facts and unambiguous philosophic arguments. In other words, he seamlessly stitches together several aspects of thought and experience to create a vision which both enthrals and instructs.

The book opens with an arresting image of deep-seated anxiety and uncertainty generated by the dream of a towering wave threatening to burst its dam and wreak havoc on the surrounding countryside. This would be particularly piquant in today's world haunted by images of destruction wrought by recurrent tsunamis and cyclones apart from human abuse and disregard of Nature. But the surging Wave symbolizes more than the threat of ecological or environmental disaster, though it is that too: it suggests anxiety generated by the churning of received beliefs and values that underpinned the European world till the other day and an intellectual and civilizational dread of further erosion of these fundamentals.

The dream, rich in layered meanings, continues within an Oxford classroom and through the battlefields of Europe; it forebodes a renewed threat to international peace after the massive death and destruction of two world wars. The "tale" about the dream arouses further speculation and anxiety and ultimately catalyses a "pilgrimage" (described as the Search) constituted by individuals who set out to explore possible answers to the conundrum. Here the reader may be forgiven for seeing a prototype in John Bunyan's *Pilgrim's Progress*, but the *Towering Wave* is not a simple moral tale: rather it is a search for a *weltanschauung*, with a complex of ideas drawn from sociology, European philosophy, history, Eastern wisdom and insights, interwoven into a poetic and visionary tapestry. This mining of Western and Eastern thoughts for responses to common human lives and conceptual problems is typical of Mallik's integrated philosophical approach (to be differentiated from the usual comparative studies).

Although decolonization has resulted in the political emancipation of the non-European world, the civilizational question must be addressed since the world's problems of thought or social order can no longer be solved — if ever they could be — solely by the internal discourse of, or international institutionalization in, Western categories. The new global situation demands that men and women of goodwill step out of the confines of the Eurocentric argument between the medieval and the modern, and take into account new challenges from the hitherto dormant or repressed civilizations of the East (Mallik's discourse was confined in his time to the Anglo-Saxon world, Europe, the USSR and Asia, but in principle would have included all) hitherto dismissed as simply "pre-modern".

However, other traditional categories also demand rethinking as the problems of conflict are universal.

In this book written in the period following the Second World War when the newly-established UNO (referred to in the book as the Conference) had inspired hopes of putting an end to war, Mallik felt constrained to point out that without a solid basis of agreement and understanding, any institution modelled on Western political practices alone would ultimately founder on the shoals of the fundamental disagreements between different peoples of the globe. And indeed only three years later the post-war peace was severely dented by the Suez crisis and the Hungarian Revolution. There has indeed as yet been no (hot) Third World War, but conflict became institutionalized in the long global Cold War stretching from 1949 (the founding of NATO) to 1989, which tolerated under its overarching umbrella of Mutually Assured Destruction, geographically limited conflagrations or proxy wars in spots like Korea, Cambodia and Afghanistan. Today we inhabit a "globalized" economically interdependent world, which again does not promise peace: apart from geographically contained wars as in the Middle East and the havoc caused by "non-state actors" the dread of another large-scale conflict has not disappeared, thanks to the persistence of received paradigms and imbalances stemming from the regroupings, readjustments and challenges emerging from the Middle East and the Asia-Pacific region. The United Nations certainly provides a forum for debates on international crises and has conducted at times contested forays into peace-keeping, but the basic flaw that went into its inception remains, that of a skewed civilizational bias. Mallik advocated searching for a system that would genuinely and equally provide accommodation for all peoples of the globe.

Despite some inevitable historical limitations of a perspective outlined six decades ago — for example Mallik's inability to anticipate the more expansionist aspects of China (though he could foresee the civilizational challenge from an emergent Asia albeit expressed today somewhat crudely in official Chinese rhetoric) or the fallout from a resurgent Middle

East, Mallik's basic philosophical–sociological insights into the nature of conflict remain relevant. Most of all his suggested approach for avoidance of conflict through the Ethics of Mutual Abstention is worthy of attention. He himself conceded that since it was based on a world-view outside what Gramsci described as the "common sense of the age" it was unlikely to be immediately accepted — but he also believed that people would be impelled in that direction when their received assumptions and values repeatedly failed to halt the apparently limitless cycle of conflict and violence. Indeed with supreme confidence *The Towering Wave* assures that the germ of the new outlook has already taken root.

Susheel Mittal of D.K. Printworld must be thanked for taking on this publishing project, and Prof. Purushottam Billimoria and Prof. Nirmalya Narayan Chakraborty for their support. Most of all one must pay homage to those dedicated British followers of Mallik, especially Winifred Lewis who after his death, worked to disseminate his works and ideas in India amongst philosophical circles and Mary M. Walker who succeeded Lewis as guardian of Mallik's legacy and became my colleague and friend. And one cannot forget Prof. Krishna Chandra Bhattacharya who consistently acknowledged Mallik's contribution, and Kalidas Bhattacharya who ran a course on his work at Shantiniketan. They form part of the small but consistent circle of Mallik's admirers.

I personally owe a debt of gratitude to M.L. Sondhi who while at Oxford in 1958 "found" Mallik's *The Individual and the Group* in a stack of unsold books under a table in Hall the Publishers. He realized he had discovered an original and significant thinker and later passed this discovery on to me.

Madhuri Santanam Sondhi

Madhuri Santanam Sondhi is author of *The Making of Peace: A Logical and Societal Framework according to Basanta Kumar Mallik* (1985) and *Martin Buber and Basanta Kumar Mallik: An Intercivilizational Dialogue on Peace* (2008). She co-edited with Mary M. Walker *Ecology, Culture & Philosophy: Metaphysical Perspectives from Basanta Kumar Mallik* (1988).

Contents

Part One

The Dream

1 The Dream

The last towering wave behind the dam gradually sloped back into the trough with boiling rage in green, black and white, and the dam stood throbbing like a vessel which has just weathered the last blow from the heaviest sea. The sigh of relief which unmistakably greeted the dam was heaved as if by the whole earth surmounted by the sky. Will the dread wave come back, will the trough boil over again and urge the wave to rise and bend the dam to its knees? This cry flooded the whole horizon.

Soon, in the breathless quiet that followed, the reply came, splitting into three distinct notes that did not coincide.

A child gave it in some long-forgotten hamlet as he assured steadily his aged and very terrified parents. With a blade of newly-cut corn in his hands he boasted that he would slay the monster when he came that evening to take his toll of lives. That was all the assurance that the hamlet got that day. The monster came as usual and the child did not survive, not to say the parents.

A city gave it while she was still in the full flush of triumph. The reply came as she was holding a banquet to celebrate the day when the élite of the new state invented the machine which could destroy the enemy for certain to establish "peace" on earth. The enemy was almost destroyed but peace never came, since the enemy returned.

A third note, a very faint whisper, seemed to reach the

vault of the sky while the crowded cities were full of riotous din. The reply that it gave was unheeded and so all its assurance that the wave had spent itself stood in the air like the glow of dawn waiting to usher in the day.

"But all this certainly is pure romancing," the Professor said, standing right inside the dream while making a rapid comment with much concern. "No such dam was ever spotted by any of our men in the field, if I am alive, nor could the earth heave a sigh of relief — nonsense — unless it all meant that there was a terrible earthquake. As for the child and the hamlet they are most certainly creations of our historians who dabble very often chiefly in art. The only part of the dream which seems to make real sense is the invention and perhaps one can even trust the whisper by way of contrast, if it ever matures into an audible claim. Till then we shall have to carry on as we have been carrying on for untold ages, whatever the result. There is no alternative to this unless we choose to perish with the halo of stupidity round our heads. It is strange that we should all still be subject to such dreams when we can truly verify facts."

The class listened to the venerable professor, all in the dream, as it had always done and not a word was said which might disturb the peace. But as they left the classroom, the students split into sections in the quad. Some said surely peace at any cost was but a lie as it was much too expensive and not worth buying. And did we ever really verify facts? The others held that since there was nothing else to be chosen in the place of this costly expensive peace one must give one's all to buy it. One could not commit suicide, one had to choose peace. There was no decision: they went back to the class day after day and repeated after the lectures the same clash of views: there was no change whatsoever in either the professor who taught or the students who wrangled.

The dream expanded and one day as it speeded on its new track suddenly the state came to a new decision about the students. The order came to the Professor that the classrooms should be removed at once to the barracks and the students should be trained in the art of warfare and not in the art of peace. Here was a big chance for them to taste what the supreme life of sacrifice meant and thereby perhaps to pave the way for eternal peace by saving meticulously what their forefathers or even unknown ancestors had in the course of ages gathered. It was not time yet for them to think, or perhaps they had been thinking too much. What was essential was that they should act to enter first into the holy spirit of tradition, the only thing which kept the celebrated mystic lore in all its fullness.

In a moment the daily wrangle after the lectures was forgotten — soon there was no trace of indecision anywhere left. What took its place for certain was a firm and great resolution on the part of the students to stand together. They felt that they saw light and were inspired by it either to give or take life. Here at last was the real universe which one could, as it were, grasp with both hands and swear allegiance to, for good and all.

And what colour and music in lavish display there came to stimulate the young spirits, or how tenaciously goodwill, sympathy and fellowship flocked from all sides to hold them firmly as they marched or flew or dived to battle, whether in the limitless vault of the sky or the unknown depth of the sea or the vast ever-expanding fields. The motto set for them was simple. "Destroy or be destroyed: seek martyrdom if you can, but do not let the good earth, for God's sake, pine for the deluge of blood." And they did destroy each other as hard as they could. They took their elders at their word. What a blessing to have elders who thought incessantly for them.

But what happened to them and their fellow students, their chief opponents, as the elders of one or the other state suddenly failed to supply the sinews of war? How did the elders themselves stand when they had to bear the brunt of the war as it suddenly swirled into their native hearth? Did they still stimulate the young when they had no time to forage history for anecdotes or martial scenes or even to seek spiritual sanctuaries to pray for help?

There was a sudden end to the fight, for it was time now, as if by schedule, that the stage should be set for justice and if possible also for a cool, calculated peace. Here was a safe return for the elders to their usual job and soon they forced the beaten enemy to confess that punishment was their due in the name of justice. They must repent by giving life or selling themselves to lifelong slavery; and when all that was done according to the code, God's earth and moral law would once again creep back to their normal places.

There was instantly peace all round, not a drop of blood was shed again. There was only the incessant cry of anguish which rises from the heart of slavery and also death which stalks in the wake of starvation, destitution and greed.

In due time the classroom was shifted back again to the old seats of learning. And as the Professor began to lecture, the students began again their wrangles in the quad. It was as if nothing had happened to them since they had gone out of their classroom to the air, the sea and the fields to give and take life as their elders wanted them to, except that the young were divided. They loved and danced, in the one state, on the village and college greens while in the other state they cursed with their heads tightly held between their knees as they squatted.

The dream here ended, like the first lesson in a Holy Service, and then the tale of it began. Strangely it was not known who let the tale of the dream out — not certainly the Professor nor the students, nor the states, since they all seemed to have lost the sense of the dream. As if they never had been in the dream. The tale, however, was somehow out and it caught on as the wild fire in the endless prairie catches on. It crept unwaveringly into every city of Europe even faster than the tales in the vast stretches of Asia or the remote wilds of Africa. What moves such tales far and wide and where the source of them lies is still unknown except perhaps to the brown and the black people of our habitable globe.

And if the white race ever had had those secrets they lost them the moment the scientific age cast a spell over all such natural upheavals in human existence. How very strange that dreams and tales about them should revive in Europe again.

This sudden revival, however, did not find its way into the record of the historians. No historian ever mentioned the dreams and the tales. It is strange how even the most profound upheavals in men's minds escape the historian! Or is it that the historian has been promise-bound to the state? Since the modern age has just passed the meridian, one must wait a while before taking any serious notice of dreams or even the more authentic phenomena of the tales about dreams. At any rate the scientist had not quite given up the claim that they were mere phantasies or brewed in the still surviving primitive cults or magic.

There were many, however, in the seats of learning who felt impelled to take a different view and these were in charge of the archives of tales and anecdotes both ancient and modern, sacred and mundane. To these authorities the tale of the dream, after a strict and judicious testing, appeared to be almost ominous though not quite diabolic. They could not dispose of it as mere myth or idle romancing. The issue was not whether it was authentic or correct. One could even pass by the claim that there was a dream. As a matter of fact these authorities forgot that the professor and his class figured only in the dream. But what they could not forget was that there was at least a tale about it, it was so vivid. And it was what this tale spread all around that upset their balance. Somehow they were deeply annoyed, perhaps even frightened. They all in a body thought they scented in it a pernicious view, one calculated to bring ruination to all that the seats of learning or the state had ever professed and heartily fostered. It really made no difference if it took the form of a dream or an idle tale or even some vapourings of mind. Who indeed was this professor? What right had he to teach the students the fatality of all things or the inevitability of events which make no room for purpose or power? Such a procedure was more than witchcraft, it was deliberate treachery or more properly a treason against the state. Or perhaps it was immaterial whether there was any such professor or his class actually corrupting the seats of learning. The fact is that the mischief had been done, once the tale of the dream had, in a weird, uncanny way, somehow got abroad. And even if the source of the tale was hidden from the public gaze, the seats of learning had to make believe that there was one. After that it should be easy according to many a hoary tradition to make a scapegoat of some and deliver society from the Evil. Could anybody for a moment deny that it was the Evil? Did it not strike at the very root of our life — our agreement to live, our holy contract with God or between man and man?

It is we who decided for all these ages in all things; and not blind fate. We do not care even for Truth. Can we live for a day if we prefer the unattainable Truth to agreement? Our forefathers concluded long ago that consistency was a virtue of the fool. To them as to us it is agreement that is the solid earth on which we live. We live and die because we have agreed that we must. We shall only perpetually die if we cease to agree. What are we coming to? Where is the commonsense of ages, the vast inheritance of the seats of learning?

2

So began the hunt, the hunt for a scapegoat, and Europe shivered in her bones.

How long was the hunt or what it produced is another story but soon a very strange thing happened. In one of the seats of learning where the leaders of thought never allowed their minds to wander too far away from what they called the immediate present, a meeting was arranged to be addressed by a man totally unknown. This seat of learning though detached by the sea from its parent stock, the original medieval seats, somehow had a taste for the unfamiliar and even occult which was suspect to the seats across the sea. It so happened that the evening when the meeting was convened fell on the close of a brilliant summer's day. The thin grey mist which the early spring had needed for maturing her buds was drawn back into the remote vault of the sky and its place was taken by the heavy spray from the blossoms which brought down the blue sky to be held in embrace by the deep green of the earth. There was complete oblivion of what it is to be in the dark, as if the night had flown from human home for ever. When, therefore, the porters of the lodge brought to the proctors the news that a strange unusual figure was going to address a meeting, and that as a matter of choice at the memorial of the martyrs, the proctors were in no mood to ban the meeting. "Who knows, it might be the medieval Christian spirit which is on the march again, why should it not?"

The evening meal was just over and as the students came out of the hall the porters told them about the meeting and the welcome which the proctors had offered to it.

It took the students only a few seconds to get to the memorial where already a large audience had gathered. But strangely enough the moment they arrived they felt they had never been to such a gathering of men and women before. There was absolute quiet, no doubt, but that was not all; everybody felt serene and peaceful and at one with everybody else which no gathering ever did in the whole history of that seat of learning. And what is more the speaker seemed to be so ancient that neither his age nor his stock could by any chance be known. No man or woman who ever lived in Europe was known to be so fantastically above age, race or tradition. And yet there was so much of quiet and penetrating vigour in all that he said. Indeed the address which he delivered could easily be in any tongue. At times it seemed he was speaking in German, French or English; at others in a Semitic tongue, Sanskrit, or Chinese. Yet the sense of all that he said was as simple, clear and inspiring as any student could ever wish it to be.

The meeting soon came to an end but strangely enough nobody had even the desire to talk to the speaker or to offer him their gratitude and respect. The speaker himself left the meeting as unobtrusively as he came but he left behind him a sense of complete satisfaction and peace.

Soon the news about what happened in the meeting got abroad. Some of the students themselves carried the news to the senior common rooms which were still debating whether the proctors were at all wise in allowing the meeting. The first reaction as the seniors received the news was one of bewilderment indeed.

What struck them most was the attitude of the students as they spoke to them. It was as if they had been to another world. Yet the strangest part of the story was that they had no account of the address given to them. They all said that they were overwhelmed by the sense of absolute peace and oneness with all. It mattered nothing to them what he spoke or in which language. They were fully convinced that they stood there before him as parts of him or he as parts of them, that they were listening to music perhaps which moulded them into unity with all. Perhaps he did not say anything, perhaps he was playing on some instrument but not for a moment did they feel that "there was a question to ask or objections to raise" or even a need to listen to a speech.

But again there is no historical record of what exactly happened to this seat of learning especially after the common rooms had fallen into a state of absolute dismay. There is no record to tell us whether a search was made to trace the strange man. From the usual familiar account which we call by the name of chronicle or history the seat of learning carried on as usual, as if nothing unusual ever happened.

But most unexpectedly the dream came back and this time it was more downright and grim. Those who were actually in the dream felt that the earth was solidly rocking to and fro as if her granite bed was giving way. Any moment it seemed she might be sucked into the bottomless pit of the surrounding vacuum. The waves clung to the earth as drowning men cling to one another. And yet there was no sense of fear, nor perhaps even a desire to live; was this the end of all existence? It was a most devastating dream.

It is not known if the Professor was in this dream but as he held forth to his class as usual there was visible sign that he was somehow rudely shaken. He looked very much greyer than ever. And the classroom, though full of habitual deference, clearly was ill at ease. It was evident that the second dream somehow had raised the issue to all concerned whether they should or could carry on as they had been carrying on for ages. What indeed was the point of it all, even if they could? Why not plunge into the vacuum itself and if possible carry on there, if carry on they must? Does it matter where they carry on if the only issue is one of carrying on and nothing else? And have they in fact only carried on so far? If they carried on for certain did they not also have to stand the shock of it all? If nothing positive was ever the yield of this eternal process of carrying on, did it not at least produce the negative? Are we not now reaching even the end of the Negative? Is not that the meaning of the dream, if it be a fact that we are not dreaming when we say that? Can we be sure even of the Negative, the perpetual torment of the body and soul?

The tale of this dream however was told in whispers; there was nothing of wild fire about it. The seats of learning felt as if the solid foundation of agreement on which all society stands like the granite bed was giving way at last. They felt as they never did before that truth has to be found since life by contract, either with God or between men, was perhaps a long illusion. If the professor was clearly wrong in insisting on the sheer fatality of things, they themselves were equally wrong in pitching their tent on the marshy soil of the sheer human will.

The dream was never forgotten nor was anything planned.

Again the historian did not record the dream, but in any case it is difficult to decide why the seats of learning so suddenly after the return of the dream lost their indomitable faith in their will force or the solid agreement to live. That meeting near the memorial of the martyrs no doubt shook them and perhaps they were tired of avoiding the truth, but the dream in which the granite base of the earth was giving way and the spectre of being sucked into the bottomless vacuum dangled before their eyes was a portent of evil. The very prospect that it drew was enough to shatter the sense of any source of strength. And the fact is that their strength was shattered. There was no sense of balance or poise anywhere left. If the bottomless void did not quite suck them into its emptiness the very image of the rocking of the earth as the granite bed was giving way made the seats of learning confused and bewildered. They became gradually incoherent, and soon they had a deep longing to save themselves by finding out the truth at any cost if possible.

Here began, without being precise as to date, the age of Conference. The dream, one may still think, was only a sign but there was no question that the seats of learning were somehow convinced by then that life by agreement and contract was a myth. It served neither man nor God. Perhaps such a myth still had some meaning but it is pointless now to cling to it. As it stands it is hollow, empty myth. If the human species has to live in the future and not be sucked into the bottomless void, the seats of learning have to discover the truth.

But what are the seats of learning going to teach the students in their present state of mind? They can still make cases on this side or on that side of any issue or claim: but that will not be teaching. To follow such a procedure is only to make a case for the sceptic or is a sheer confession of failure. The students have to be taught and not confused if the seats of learning have to preserve themselves. They have to be given guidance and be put with reference to the past in a position where they can either rediscover the past or go in advance of it. But if the past is a conundrum, surely students who are yet to be initiated into the main trend of history cannot be given a conundrum as if it was the main trend. Better far would it be to give them a long holiday than to bewilder them by presenting them with a clean vacuum in the place of truth and guidance.

Fortunately the long vacation soon arrived at such a critical moment for the seats of learning. It was a great relief.

It is another matter what life the students were going to live at home, since like their teachers they too had undergone a terrific change as a result of the dreams or the tales about them. Let us follow for the moment the career of the teachers as the vacation began.

Usually the vacation is the time for them to go out cruising on the seas or climbing mountains or exploring distant climes with their strange manners and customs or spending a part of the vacation in examining papers or preparing lectures for the Michaelmas term. All these usual ways of relaxation or fresh experience had by now lost their appeal. They really did not know what to do with their time. Indeed these vacant days would have been a very serious problem to the seats of learning if they had not had a sudden call from the state to join the Conference.

It was strange that the Conference should coincide exactly with the long vacation. It seemed as if something unusual was happening all the time. This call was indeed a godsend to them; it held out at least the only remaining chance of reviewing the whole position in history if that was still possible.

The fact was that while the seats of learning had been rudely shaken by the two successive dreams, the states had lost completely their usual sense of power and strength after the two world wars they had recently fought. While the dreams challenged the serenity of thought by exposing the inner working of events behind the façade of deliberate thought, the wars exposed the hollowness of the political creed that the state can by the sheer act of will control the human mind. If there was confusion in the seats of learning, there was chaos in the field where the drama of action is played. The disillusionments came together, as if by some strange Cosmic plan.

But what really held the states at this hour was nothing if not a deep sense of dread slowly but steadily rising to the level of panic. No doubt the two wars and the long preparation for them had preceded the dread, but they did not quite account for it. Nobody knew why or how it came; its real origin could not possibly be traced. And perhaps as a result of this deep sense of dread the states stood as if they were mere skeletons of glorious days — at least the burning faith which at one time filled them was completely gone. Instead, as the historians recorded carefully, what looked like a deluge of iron and steel swamped them the moment the two wars had come to an end. It was difficult even to see after that where they belonged or what they had been. Report has it that they found themselves suddenly driven back to the remote atomic age long past the metal or stone ages of prehistoric times — an age, perhaps, in which even the blade of grass refused to sprout.

The states had fallen into this dubious frame of mind before ever the Conference seriously began.

The dread, however, arose, by all the records, in the same way as the dreams had arisen; the states suddenly felt that the Dark Age which they thought they had crushed for ever might any day return with a fresh challenge, or the spirit of stark revenge might inexorably cross over the seven seas from the distant lands of the Far East and take back all the treasures it had lost to the European states. There was no faith left which was capable of keeping this dread out once it had arisen.

Curiously, while the loss of faith coincided inevitably with the sense of dread, the rapid growth of the machine age brought them a fresh conceit as if to compensate for that loss. The states in consequence oscillated between nervousness and dread, which made them prone to seek a solution in a real meeting between states, and a mood to derive security by ruthless destruction which the machine made them believe they could easily achieve: as if half the time the states behaved as rational human agents and half the time as mere puppets in the hands of the machine. And this constant oscillation proved to be so intense a strain on their nerves that they had to cultivate openly what they called the "cold war" or "war of nerves" if only to convince their own inner souls that they really were safe or not wholly in the wrong. Or at times, when they followed the machine like flocks of sheep without counting the cost, they reduced whole countrysides to devastation by ruthless destruction. And then instantly they assured themselves, as one lost in a dream, that they would repent if necessary by the resurrection of all that they had destroyed.

As every historian knows, the states have been ruthless more often than not in their long history of deeds. Only yesterday life was destroyed with a cool and calculating design. Still, somehow there was a purpose behind all that destruction, however grim, and even the pathetic faith that no life would have to be destroyed again in the limitless future of the race. That was absolutely the last time that life was to be done to death by design or force as the case in question required.

But this time, in the presence of the dread, not even the semblance of an ideal inspired the states. There could be no purpose in a machine especially when it is in the hands of states in which men are filled with a sense of dread. There could only be reckless speed, which might easily be cold and inhumanly cruel.

3

It was exactly in such a dubious frame of mind that the states decided that they should all meet and by close deliberation find a way out of perpetual struggle. They also made up their minds that no creed whether of tradition, caste or colour should be allowed to dictate about the range or structure of the basis of that meeting. Let all races and cultures come and find out at least what really was wrong in the human family. Let there be frank and open exchange of views whether about common essential interests or just grievances and let nothing restrain them except the necessity that in giving expression to their views they may not lost sight of the dread which like a vast shadow is hanging over them. No historian forgot to note that the meeting was proposed not in the usual spirit of political mind but with a frank spontaneity which at least the sense of dread induced.

Evidently the venue of the Conference had to be planted in the city, since it was the city which marked the home of the modern age. Perhaps such conferences never were held either in the medieval or the classical past — the issue for decision in those days was different and the ancient or medieval cities were certainly not symbols of what are known as "process" or "progress" today. A conference, again, has no resemblance to the meeting of the princes for decision in the court of God by trials of ordeal and combat. It marks, on the contrary, an attempt by man to decide without the aid from any precedent from the past or from holy guidance. Its origin lies in a state of confusion and its main quest is truth and not a mere reformulation of the desire to live. And so it does not mark merely the common agreements but seeks to register an absolute truth. And if the modern city alone can serve as its venue, the reason is that the city as we know it is not the heart of a state but only a "process" or "movement". It never really stands but runs perpetually through the two processes of being built and destroyed. As a symbol of modern life which is incessant change, it alone could provide a basis for the confusion on which the meeting between the modern states in conference arose. There would be no conferences today if the cities were not there.

And it is by no means strange that the members also of the Conference, the states themselves, should appear to partake more of the nature of a process than what is called static poise. Whether as nations or societies of men and women which outran their natural bounds they seemed to change their groupings everyday rather than to abide by professions solemnly rendered. No value seemed to have a hold on them except that of sheer preservation of self and that meant in its turn only the right or chance to live by satisfying mostly the economic need. Or more precisely, as they had lost all faith and were constantly in dread of losing life itself, they never could abide by any promise given or taken. They rather oscillated between chances and built on expectations which had no precedent to justify them. The states, cities and conferences were all of one piece and consistency.

But what happened on the eve of the Conference when the states and the seats of learning met? What could happen if neither of them brought to it anything but vacant minds and a deep sense of frustration which the dreams in the one case and the wars in the other brought about?

Could a mere meeting of the states or the seats of learning produce as if by magic the truth or even throw some fresh light on it? How much of truth came out of the long past of mere herding together of men in the towns and villages, and the animals and the trees in the forest zones? Yet, even a chance meeting between travellers on the open road as they sat and talked in the lonely hut or wayside inn or under a spreading tree is reputed to have solved the problems of human life. The reason was that the travellers were out on the open road with a definite purpose and so sparks flew as soon as they met. No doubt states must meet as men do before they could find out anything they want to find out. Neither men nor states can grasp the truth if they have truly lost the art of meeting. Life after all is meeting if it is anything. But the meeting must take place under the right auspices in which to produce results and these mean at least the right goal or objective and a chastened spirit which believes in truth, the equality of all human needs and the necessity of realizing them. Such meetings do not take place in the marketplace nor in the chamber of deputies where men meet to outdo one another in the skilled art of deception or brow-beating as the occasion demands. If you are interested in making profit you cannot possibly find the truth but you will make only profit with the certainty of losing it later. And profit is made and lost when there are goods to sell and buy. Still, you may sell and buy goods and yet not make a profit and from this trade you will not keep away if you have discovered in time that there is nothing to gain in making profit.

"But all this sounds like a sermon from a pulpit," the seats of learning said in a chorus. "Where indeed is the truth to be found? Why mention it then?"

"True, the truth has to be found, since it is not there yet, but why indeed did the seats of learning come to the

Conference if they really wanted only to start debates? The seats of learning must remember that they had nothing to say for themselves after the dreams had shaken them to their roots. Did they think the states asked them to join the Conference only to be regaled by their old varsity habit of merely talking or writing to no effect?" Somewhere in the Conference a voice spoke out like this.

The Conference, however, was held and some said the other day that it is still being held and will continue to be held, even if it does not lead to any result. But the Conference certainly at this early stage is in its juvenile form; it could not for instance be expected to supersede all at once the modes of settling differences hitherto followed by the states. Even warfare though on a minor scale might be carried on in one sphere of the states while the Conference was being held in another. Some noted authority, again, in the seats of learning, might spin out theories in the Conference chamber by speech after speech; some other equally noted authority in the vast expanse of states might instantly proceed to test that theory on the field of battle. If the theory was true it should, they might argue, stand the shock of any challenge for verification or proof. Many other things might happen, too, which the early youth of the Conference easily permitted. The technique of running its procedure, for instance, might be a ready-made instrument instead of being a fluid process left to chance. Even if it had to be austerely democratic and not by any chance autocratic, its form in terms of majority or even unanimity might be offered to the Conference in a ready-made shape. Why not? Instead of leaving it to what the ancients called rhetoric, or weak will or shady practices, the whole technique might be produced in a committee of sane and honest men who would weigh every pro and con. And why should not such committees be appointed when the states and the seats of learning had met as partners in a common pursuit? It was sheer waste of time, they might think, to let every man or woman speak. Better far to rationalize their views in advance and shape them according to rules.

This was, at least, the emphatic view of some of the states which loudly stood for peace and called it at times by the name of pure democracy. The Conference indeed was in its juvenile phase.

The truth was that nobody knew what the technique for a Conference truly was, just as they had no idea what a Conference was. And so it was by no means strange that they should run the democratic technique as if it was a dead horse. The result, in consequence, was not movement in the shape of frank and open speech in the debate that followed but dead unanimity which rose from deep and uncanny silence. One could hardly give expression to one's opinion since the ubiquitous dead horse invariably choked one's voice. In fact, nobody had the chance to speak out.

Even the voices that still somehow managed to sound were drowned in silence or seemed to come from the street outside or from the sea that was waiting patiently to carry the carcass of the dead horse away.

It was simply not seen in the early stages of the Conference that neither the democratic nor the autocratic technique was of any use to it since such techniques needed the genuine autocrats or democrats to run them. If by any chance the pure autocratic or democratic spirit could be revived in the Conference, the techniques in question could be of real use to it. But such a revival would have killed outright the prospect of holding the Conference. The modern city, again, in its restless form, if it was the right venue for the Conference by virtue of the fact that it alone by breeding confusion made conferences possible, was not a suitable place in which the true autocrat or democrat could work in peace. The city, it seemed, had passed even the stage of hybrid politics. What was prevailing all round was the politics of dread and fear from which normally policy and faith most scrupulously disappear.

And that is the chief reason why the technique which the early stage of the Conference followed was regimented voting, a strange mixture in which freedom and authority struggled hard to drown each other to death. Neither the classical nor the medieval model could any longer be of use and since there was no other model known in tradition, the Conference had to make believe that their mixture did really produce a model. There was no alternative to it since the birth of a new technique presupposed the birth of truth itself. The states had to follow as a matter of course the lead of what was sheer habit and ignorance.

But this did not necessarily mean that the Conference began with a fatal handicap and was from its inception much too weak to escape disaster. Mere habit and ignorance cannot by themselves ruin a Conference; the occasion for real crisis for any gathering arises if habit or ignorance is the sole means of realizing a fresh and potent ideal. If by any chance the Conference had begun with a preconceived goal and if there was no means of realizing it except what was guaranteed by sheer habit and ignorance it could not possibly have avoided a crisis or a disaster. If nothing else, the regimented voting itself would have shattered its chances for ever.

But the states did not come to the Conference with any ideal or goal. Their most pressing need was to discover a goal by which they could all stand united and remove the all-encompassing dread. If there was anything ruling the spirit of the Western states at the time it was the dread of the return of the Dark Age and the onrush of the mystical East across the seas. Such a state of mind cannot create a crisis, not to say warfare. A war presupposes a faith, at least some definite objective. It may be waged for wrongs suffered, for the reinstatement of dignity that was lost or for the spread of a new faith which will bring about that reinstatement. A mere sense of insecurity, which follows inevitably days of prosperity, is still a sign of faith, not of doubt which undermines faith. And the more acute this sense becomes in the nature of things, the more liable to dreams the nation which suffers from it is bound to be. The Conference, therefore, with habit and ignorance for its mainspring of action was ripe for a third dream but not for a third war.

And so it did not come to any serious harm since it could not. And it made no difference if the Conference actually behaved at times as if it was only a stage for a drama and not a parliament. Even its meaningless behaviour in this early stage was almost a prelude to some good which inevitably followed. The statesmen who led the Conference had to play out the techniques they were familiar with before they could be in a position to realize how antiquated indeed these were. They had to fail completely before they could realize how incompetent they were to run the Conference: and it was only then that the Conference could be expected to yield the real ideal and the technique relevant to it. The fact was that the result of the huge waste of time in regimented voting was the conclusion that the immediate need of the Conference was a thorough review of the past as a preliminary to any construction. It came to be agreed sooner or later that nothing of any consequence could be done in the Conference so long as the present enigmatic situation had not been thoroughly traced to its relevant past.

There was really nothing seriously wrong with the states or the seats of learning except that they did not know how to change easily their old habits of thought and action — it would be foolish to suggest that these habits undermined even their eagerness to preserve themselves. And it is a fact that they could not account for their sense of dread which took an unaccountable form. It was only yesterday that they had the grim experience of two devastating wars. Besides, it was a riddle to them why the two dreams which followed in rapid succession should have so completely unbalanced the seats of learning. Even the two wars, however devastating, were not sufficient to account for the dread in that definite form or for the loss of faith in their sense of power and strength. And it really made no difference if they behaved in the early stage of the Conference without any sense of proportion, as if they were stars shooting across the tense horizon of political suspense. All that was but an evidence, if anything, of their extreme anxiety to get the state of riddle solved. It was no longer possible for them to carry on as they had been carrying on so long as riddles stared them in the face like the sphinx of old.

4

Soon, therefore, a committee was formed to go into the whole question of review, with a thorough analysis of the past which had led up to the present. And the preliminary issue before the committee was to decide two important points: if the review of the past had to be made before the discovery of truth fell due, how far back into the past should such a review run? And who, again, was competent to undertake the review or what were the conditions the reviewer must satisfy before a claim could be made on his behalf?

With regard to the second issue it was at once agreed that none of the states or the seats of learning that advised them could be trusted to undertake that review. Evidently they were much too absorbed in their own specific interests to take a really detached view of the past. Besides, the conditions for such a review meant that the reviewer must not only be above any sectional claim but somehow must be convinced that there was nothing to choose between one sectional claim and another. Finally, the detachment which neutrality in such a case implied was not a mere matter of standing on the common faith or ground which the states in conflict might still somehow be found to imply. Since the reviewer had to trace the origin of the past, he might be compelled to leave the standpoint of what has been known as the common ground, or faith in history. The issue was by no means simple. Perhaps so far in history there had been nothing held in common by all the states or seats of learning; perhaps the real common ground had to be found outside the pale of history altogether.

And this at once revealed to the committee the answer to the question how far back into the past the reviewer had to go. If the issue was one of reaching a common ground in the past which could be accepted by all, that past could not be traced in history in the way in which our historians have so far traced it. An altogether new account of the past may have to be found, a past which no historian perhaps ever dreamt of. Indeed it may be necessary to raise even the issue of genesis again.

The report of the committee, therefore, could hardly be assuring to the Conference as a whole, and some of the impatient members felt at once that they would much rather trust their "machine" and bring about quick results instead of waiting on the proceeds of a wild-goose chase. "After all, our learned and wise men," they suddenly said, "do not exactly produce the guns, or even food; and what indeed have they to show after centuries of thinking? Perhaps it was they who always put grit in the machine, or how is it that it is only in the twentieth century that the machine is working wonders, and may any day beat the so-called achievement of the miracles?" This was the reaction to the report from the "Machine" states as they were called.

And these states, which believed in action when it was wholly led by machine, would have won the day and broken up the committee for good if one or two states had not intervened to point out to them two salient facts against this claim:

First, machine is a game at which more than one can play, and even if one side gains control over it and realizes their immediate goal, there is no certainty that the other side may not relieve them of that control sooner or later; so that the fact that action or machine can achieve quick results is of no avail to the family of states. It is really of no avail even to a state which is determined to win here and now, no matter what its posterity might have to pay. Such a state is the common enemy of the family of states as much as of its own posterity.

Second, no machine, again, ever functioned without either destroying its opposite number or being destroyed by it. Somehow, there is a duality of machine as there is a duality of everything else including human claims and motives. Everything appears in a dual form of contrariety. No machine ever worked except for a time and then it had to bear the brunt of Nemesis.

Where, then, is the guarantee that the machine which is all-powerful today will not be challenged by its opposite number sooner or later, and that disastrously.

The states fell into a complete quandary again, and the Conference, it seemed, had no longer a *raison d'être* for continuing its course. The Machine States, all visibly impatient, had to relieve this tension by precipitating one or two minor events with or without the consent of the other states. And this ominous break led gradually to a split in the Conference clearly indicating the close of its early stage. It was not possible that with its present mood and equipment the Conference could possibly achieve anything of any real use or value.

Still its total achievement was not nil since it cleared the air considerably by emphasizing the need of a review and showing how that review fell beyond the capacity of the seats of learning or the statesmen of the traditional type. Besides it also happened that the Machine States did not succeed in gaining quick results and were practically at their wits' end about any future plan. There was a lot of destruction done, no doubt, but no forest is without a daily round of slaughter and still the forest survives.

One thing was certain, the split between the states, once it appeared, steadily widened. As if a real Armageddon might soon begin and the dread which stood like a thick coat of fog over the whole panorama might for a moment recede. Everything seemed to be at the mercy of events; and soon the states arrayed themselves in forms which seemed to have no point in common.

But strangely, as the dread would have it, even such a change in the relation between the states had its value since the states in the West in the twentieth century did not know what the Dark Age really was or what the spirit of the East truly implied. They had strong convictions, no doubt, on any issue professed; and they judged the Medieval in their continental home and the true Asian in the Far East in terms of their own professions. There was only one clear standard or ideal for them; the rest of life whether in the remote or recent past or the surrounding present was but a partial copy of it. It was certainly necessary for them that they should see what at least the Far East was in her true historical shape and form. That seemed to be almost the cosmic reason why the split between the states should have arisen as it did.

For the first time for centuries the East stood out again instead of being somewhere merged in the penumbra of the West. It soon appeared that the main question was not whether, for instance, Medievalism and Humanism should prevail one over the other or would necessarily in their present form have to live together. The seats of learning and the "men of the states" were quite mistaken in posing the main issue in that form. The main issue was the ultimate clash between the East and the West and perhaps it was this clash that underlay the dread of the Dark Age or of the Far East which neither the states nor the seats of learning could escape.

Soon it came to be apparent to all but a few that the states in the West widely differed from the states in the East. The two major states in the East, for instance, stood for peace and dignity, while the one which somehow embodied in itself both the East and the West stood for justice. Nobody could miss these obvious facts except when subconscious statecraft or cold war clouded the sky.

The states of the West, on the other hand, stood for security, a security which did not necessarily count its cost to others not included in their social scheme. The others had yet to stand to the Western states on terms of equality and so, by a curious logic, security for them did not exactly mean the same thing as the Western states took their own security to mean. And it was equally natural that they would miss the significance of justice, and find it meaningless to stand for peace and dignity in the way in which the two states in the East wholeheartedly did. Not that they did not want peace and had no use for dignity as ideals or objectives in their own schemes but the dread which held them as in a vice forced them to make security their only value at the moment. And so they did not, for instance, build or construct in the West except to repair damages or to remove the inequalities in their domestic life, the deposit of ages. And if perchance they had the means of building on a large scale they built the ramparts of defence with their long flying arms to crush the enemy at a distance. No other type of building was possible for them since the dread prevailed; and it did prevail in at least one of the states in such a form as seemed to pass all bounds.

The states in the East or in the steppe land between the East and the West, on the other hand, had a different programme. They too had to build up a defence, since the Conference of states produced no evidence that the obstacles to their preservation or progress were a myth; they were still exposed to dangers as they had been for centuries, though not on the same scale as before. The habit or inertia which sustained the modern imperial creed still operated although it had lost its primal force. The main part of the programme of construction in the East, therefore, was to repair the damage of a long past and bring the people to a condition where they would really begin after centuries to live in peace and with dignity.

But how was it that still the East filled the West with dread? Why should the West take the East in her attempt to build for peace, dignity and justice as the only real obstacle in their way? Did they not value their own dignity and claim to have worked for peace in the past when they had the chance?

The fact was that the issue of the split between the East and the West was not that of peace and preservation or dignity and security or justice and domination, as it appeared to be to many in the West. The issue, indeed, was very much deeper and it was this ultimate fact which the appearance of the split disclosed. It was gradually seen that perhaps the East and the West did not by any chance mean by peace and dignity exactly the same thing. There was on the contrary a world of difference between the way of life which the East cherished and that which the West upheld. Such ways as are embodied in their respective social schemes might even be opposites; and as opposites they are bound to clash. Finally, an accurate review of history might even reveal the fact that the East and the West never worked together in the whole course of their existence although no historian so far has had the courage or wisdom to point this out.

It follows, therefore, that in no way could one condemn the Conference of the states as sheer waste of time and funds. Even the procedure in it was not altogether in vain; at least the committee that it set up to diagnose the past was both judicious and firm in pointing out the incapacity of the states and the seats of learning to undertake that review. If nothing else was done, it led at any rate to the statement and formulation of the problem before the world today.

The problem is to resolve the split between the East and West and not to make believe that there really is no split. The states cannot again revert to their imperial role which refused to recognize the split; and even if such reversion does occur by the pressure of sudden increase in their wealth, it will be short-lived and ultimately quicken the pace of resolution. An increase in wealth without an ideal to distribute it is a sure sign of decay.

But why should not the committee then resume its sittings if the problem is so clear? Why should it not start an analysis of the split, if the relationship between the East and the West does really indicate a split? Even if one grants that the seats of learning were not qualified to advise the states in undertaking a review of the past, it does not follow that they were equally unqualified to undertake an analysis of the split. At least they were fully familiar with what is implied by the notion of split. It would be stupid to suggest that the seats of learning never went beyond the stage of contradiction in their analysis of conflict and so did not know what opposites or incompatibles meant. It is a commonplace of history that schools of thought divided the seats of learning on the ground of the importance they attached respectively to the notions of the dialectic and creation as theories bearing on the true origin of things. While the medieval school of thought meticulously made the universe free from the contagion of the opposites in the interest of the merciful purpose of God, the later modern school supported the dialectic by ruling out any outside influence in its course.

But it so happened that the seats of learning drew a line

between the issue of opposition in its ultimate metaphysical sense and that of its form on the sociological plane. They could not see that the relation of opposition between the East and the West if it was a fact was one of contrariety; they did not believe they were strict opposites. In other words they were not prepared to recognize the East as equal partners with the West in any relationship, whether of harmony or conflict, with the same prospects for failure as for success. At any rate, no European tradition has hitherto recognized a standard or value which could be a rival to his own however pathetic this may sound. There has been naturally many a strange instance. The mystical East, for example, was granted by the orthodox European the credit of having unconsciously worked out the Christian gospel or the Platonic Idea. So Gautama the Buddha was given a niche in the hierarchy of saints in the Catholic Church. In exactly the same spirit was the latest figure on the Indian stage acclaimed by the Christian world as either a very near relation of Jesus Christ or by a strange divine dispensation the only devout Christian left in the benighted milieu of the modern world. It was only the other day, again, that a very ardent Christian missionary went the length of sacrificing himself for his faith in the intimate environment of Gandhi and Tagore. And the result inscrutably was that while he died in India after a lifelong devotion to them, still proclaiming his faith in Jesus, it did not strike either Gandhi or Tagore that they should accept the Christian creed if only as a mark of hospitality to their devoted Christian neighbour. It was not possible that the European could accept the relation between the East and the West as one of equal partnership whatever the issue or occasion. Nor would the East for a like reason accept the West on equal terms when she would have the full chance of rising to her normal stature. We are here face to face with the nemesis of history.

5

What exactly happened at this stage of the European situation when the split steadily widened can be gathered from a vivid account which two non-Europeans put on record after a visit to Europe during this critical period. These visitors met in an Asian city in the house of a mutual friend and it was here that they had the chance to fully relate their experiences to a highly sophisticated body of people. The house was well known for such gatherings, though the evening on which this extremely interesting talk took place had been set apart for an informal meeting. It marked the last day of a festival.

One of the visitors said:

> The most curious feature of the European situation today is that while the Western mind will not recognize the split between the East and the West although it is a plain, obvious fact, it is constantly coming up against the phenomenon in almost every avenue of its domestic politics. No major European state is free from a conflict of interests in its internal politics today, a conflict which can be described only in terms of a split. Whatever the significance of the party system in their political scheme the parties are to-day standing out as frank opposites. It may at least be argued that sooner or later the whole of parliamentary government on which the party system stands might like an applecart be completely upset. And what would happen to the state itself after that is an open question. Some at least say it will

> wither away for sheer absence of a common purpose or of the background of unity; and the evidence they give refers to the fact that while one of the parties is seeking to ally itself with an outside state at the expense of its complete sovereignty the other party is getting internationally minded, which means seeking an alliance with a state that repudiates national sovereignty. Politically the situation is most obscure and unstable.

The other visitor while fully agreeing with the first speaker told the gathering that exactly the same phenomenon of split was seen operating in the relationship between the states themselves.

> It is a fact that ever since the split between the East and the West has appeared, the states as a matter of sheer necessity have spared no pains to consolidate their common agreement. They have met with great expectations in many a fraternal gathering and have solemnly declared that whatever happened they would abide by their common descent and preserve the immortal legacies which they have inherited from their common ancestry. Even some of the oldest of the scholars in Europe have met in such political gatherings to vouchsafe for the urgency of such a need, at the cost of lifelong profession. It is difficult to believe that there is any trace of the acute differences between, say, a humanist and a medievalist, or a Tory and a Socialist on this common platform.
>
> But invariably after all this solemn declaration of unity they have been caught up as if by fate in ominous clashes the moment they came to safeguarding their national interests. Whether on economic issues or matters of defence, especially where some remnant of imperial interest still survives, they cannot see eye to eye. The issue at once arises whether the interests of European unity can in the last analysis be reconciled with the interests of national existence. The issue remains today undecided. Here, therefore, is a split again. It seems as if the Fates are following on their heels.

At this stage, after the two visitors had spoken, one of the gathering who was a noted historian thanked them for their most valuable comments on modern European life and then drew a comparison between modern Europe as a community of men and women and medieval European civilization which lasted with its own structure of society for at least a thousand years. The point that he made was that since Europe in its modern structure has been an aggregation of states, it cannot be changed into a unity of the medieval pattern, however much this is desired. But this is exactly what the states of Europe in their aggregated form seem to be trying to achieve. The nation states cannot be liquidated; nor can a unity whether holy or secular be introduced in their place unless the prospect of a revival of the medieval age has actually arisen. Even the unification of the states by force under the hegemony of one state — a pale imitation of the Roman model — cannot be repeated. And the recent theory of Federation, which means splitting the two features — the boundaries of the states and their functions — is already almost in a hopeless quandary. Perhaps there is only one more experiment which can still be made, on the basis of a hegemony of raw materials concentrated in the hands of one state, but it will not avoid the return of the split sooner or later.

The two visitors were greatly impressed with the historian, especially as they saw now why indeed the European states seemed to them to be living from day-to-day without any policy or principle, as if they were at the sheer mercy of events. It was difficult indeed, they said, not to believe that the events were happening as a result of some hidden hostility to the European states on the part of evil forces. Or how was it that a just and honourable King should suddenly fall ill and die in the midst of all the extreme international uncertainty: would not many of us take it as a bad omen? Or elections should have to be precipitated in the leading states as if to plant the seed of revolution in the heart of constitutional politics. The states had to turn aside from the grave international problems under these stresses and devote all their energies to dealing with the sudden dislocation of the nation's primary needs. "These are inexplicable phenomena indeed, unless one accounts for them in the light of the one supreme phenomenon, that the split had appeared between the East and the West. I do not want to appeal for evidence," the visitor said, "to the occult and mystical but it is difficult not to do so at times."

Yet could one really account for the devastating floods and droughts in Europe while the embers of the Second World War were still leisurely smouldering, or the sudden undreamt-of fall of avalanches on the long-settled and prosperous human homes in the modern age of Europe when at every turn of life it was the scientific leadership which was ostentatiously proclaimed to the utter shame and dismay of any other ever known? Where indeed was Nature in the modern age unless she was cribbed, cabined and confined under the rigid and strict control of the scientist in his far-flung, well-built laboratory? Could the floods and droughts possibly appear in broad daylight in the mid-twentieth century to wreck human homes mercilessly without the scientist's tacit consent? It almost seems as if we are at last reaching the anticlimax of the scientific age; and perhaps it may even have dawned on the scientist himself that, after all, his much vaunted theory of the universe and the technique which he has fashioned so energetically on the anvil of that theory was but a gift to him from Nature herself. If both his repertoire and ritual consisted in nothing but plain and simple "observation" and the "uniformities" it has from time to time yielded — we need not complicate matters by bringing in the mathematician — he was obviously at the mercy of Nature. He was like a man on the watchtower whose job was to report the clouds and the flood, the drought and the crashing avalanche. The real spring and fountainhead of them were elsewhere — remote from the laboratory so fondly cherished; and if still some credit has to be reserved for the scientist for all his pains to serve humanity, the consent for the award has to come from Nature herself and not the laboratory. And, who knows, the scientist may still be open-minded enough to consider that perhaps Nature was not altogether worshipped in vain.

The occult and the mystical, according to the visitors, may not be quite out of the picture yet. Either there may be a resurgence or revival of them or an altogether new way of prospecting the future may be found. The conclusion is that the situation in Europe is abnormal to anyone unless he or she is fatally obsessed with the eternity of the modern state or science in Europe.

At this stage it was the host of the gathering who referred to the honest European effort long before the split appeared, to solve the issue of world peace by what was described as the League of Nations. The host was perhaps the oldest member of the gathering and had sufficient experience to review the whole history of the European situation from the First World War to the appearance of the split which took place after the Conference had to all intents and purposes failed. He pointed out that the League of Nations came to nothing for one simple reason: the nations outside the European family could not be assimilated as either "copies" or "potencies" of the European family. They remained as they were in spite of the League — unique and original experiments in the social evolution of mankind. It was ridiculous to believe, as the European mind honestly did, that the rest of the hemisphere was but an extension of the continent of Europe. There was the classic example of Rhodes who failed to draw the line of the boundary of Europe short of the eternal stars. And how the stars hated the approach of Rhodes! The attempt of Gobineau, again, which was in the opposite key, was by no means more successful than that of Rhodes. He was correct about splitting the "stocks" but the result was not a hierarchy but a dialectic, the evidence for which is now vividly present in the split. Where is Rhodes now? And where is Gobineau? And where is Gobineau's successor, Hitler, who had to take poison to escape his tribulations on earth?

Europe, today, is to all appearance a ramshackle civilization. If she is not heading for the cruel aftermath which followed the sack of the Roman Empire she will find it very difficult to escape the consequences of her completely inept way of managing her affairs.

Or how is it that, at a moment when the dread of a collapse or steady decline has got them all in its firmest grip, the European states should still be carrying on in their daily existence in the same old way as if nothing had ever happened to disturb that way. If they are not fighting among themselves each one of them is fighting in domestic concerns. It seems at times that there is no sense in them of the necessity to husband every ounce of their strength for their main fight with the East, which, according to them, threatens their vital interest. Where is the good, one might argue, of manufacturing atom bombs to destroy the enemy when not a shred of unity or a common inspiration happens to bind the people of the states together? If they not only distrusted one another but lived in mortal dread when passions ran high in their domestic behaviour would they have the will left in them when the time comes for throwing the bomb at the distant enemy? The issue invariably arises at such moments — "who is my enemy" — almost as a parody on the saying "who is my neighbour?"

The Conference practically ceased to function after it had produced the sense of the real split between the East and the

West — its main achievement. And the committee that sat to analyse the conditions for an adequate review naturally ended. It could not recommend the seats of learning or the statesmen of the old school as competent experts for that review.

The situation in Europe was tense and enigmatic: in it the split between the East and West was the outstanding fact even as the sense of insecurity in the Western states was painfully vivid. And it was evident that the seats of learning had practically nothing to suggest to remove the split. If they had some energy left when they came to the Conference at the bidding of the states, the events which marked the early phase of the Conference left them practically speechless. Some of the members in consequence were openly or quietly leaving the seats of learning and entering, as of old, into holy places or sanctuaries. At any rate the atmosphere in the realm of thought was painfully unsteady. The Professor was still there, no doubt, with his classroom, which opened after the Long Vacation. But as the seats of learning partially dispersed and the students were again called upon by the states to be trained in the art of defence, nobody took any special interest in what the professors taught or how the students reacted to their teaching. The students were mostly busy passing examinations, since at least the economic pressure was steadily growing on them all. And if the quest of truth survived in the shape of what is called specialization and research it did not matter what subject one chose or what the research on it produced. When the best that any professor could inspire his students to produce only served the life of the community from day-to-day, public interest in the work of the seats of learning rose or fell in the same way as it did in the share market, or the yield of agriculture or transport, or the football pool, or parliamentary skill in debate and many other such interests which keep the daily life going The seats of learning really had nothing to teach on the main issues; the professor in his laboratory could only carry on and the students just lived from day-to-day. Europe was not in a position to produce anything but bombs or cars or sheer movements in colour, shape or sound or just huge, sheer proportions in height. It seemed as if the sky, the earth and the sea would all be drawn together soon into one steady whirlpool of movement. Perhaps the last scene on the modern European stage would enact a vast adieu to Time from Space and then what would happen it is left entirely to the imagination to portray.

The most curious phenomena, however, in the midst of all this diverse "movement" were the establishment of the "welfare state" and a review of history in the shape of an Exhibition of the age of industry, science and art. The review was very bold indeed and seemed to be in a mood to put back the whole trend of history, if possible. As if Truth, Beauty and Plenty appeared only in the stages which lead up necessarily to anarchy and confusion. The grim phenomena which followed in the wake of this so-called growth were either not known or carefully weeded out. It was the thrush that came into the picture as it sat on the top of the elm and sang to give thanks to the God of the Universe — the poor worm on which he dined that evening was forgotten. What indeed is the good of building a "welfare state" when it is not known what is meant by "welfare" or "state"? If the young are fed, housed and clothed as they never were before, what is meant by this sudden respite from hunger, shivering and suffering when it is certain that they sooner or later will be slaughtered like well-fed cattle on the field of battle? If the seats of learning had nothing to teach them except conundrums or gospels which led to warfare, why bring them up in a "welfare state" at all? Why are they trained and taught to value prospects when there are no such prospects, as the seats of learning to their own dismay have long ago realized? The irony is that the "welfare state" is perhaps the cruellest technique ever propounded to fill the life of youth with shame, misery and anguish which the youths of old, bred in poverty, never knew. Did the monks wed poverty for nothing? Did the youths of old only suffer? One wonders if even the horrors of modern warfare would compare unfavourably with the "welfare state", since the latter, it seems, stands naked like the King of Cobras erect on its victim in the forest.

6

It was really high time that the third dream arrived; it was anxiously awaited to relieve the tension. But it did not arrive though the air was tense. But something suddenly did arrive; it was not a dream but simply the strange, unfamiliar light from the mystical world.

One day, in the Far East, in the very heart of it, a most uncommon event happened. A steady, firm voice from the depths of the mystical world gave out that the way of life which was Truth was no longer cast in shadows but already actually known to the human mind. It was a direct message and came in the shape of an utterance by a living Mystic, it was impossible to miss it. It was not a vision that needed interpretation, or a word spoken by a hidden spirit, or a gesture or sign in the sky, or a dream that required to be read. It was the message from a Mystic and he quietly indicated the place where the way of life could be found.

It is not the usual practice where such events still happen in the twentieth century to ask questions or make inquiries. It is strictly the hour for receiving messages, quietly delivered. And it so happened that those who had the privilege of receiving that message were born and bred in such environment and took this sudden, unexpected message as a revelation to them.

Apparently the source of its authority lay in the long persistent age of mysticism and the credit of the Mystic himself who delivered it. The utterance of the Mystic was a miracle to those who received it and it will reverberate through all the ages of eternity.

Part Two

The Vision

1 The Vision

As there was a hunt for the scapegoat after the tale of the first dream got abroad — though there is no record of it — there was inevitably a quest for the Truth after the mystic had indicated the exact place where it was to be found. There is again no historical record of the quest. Such a quest was bound to arise since the states and the seats of learning especially in the Western world seemed to be drifting steadily towards the edge of confusion.

It is another issue where and how exactly this quest arose and how far down in men's minds its roots lay. Perhaps that will never be known till the historian has realized that the record he has been keeping for centuries has merely scraped the surface of human experience. Only there is some evidence that the people who joined in the quest were aware that many men and women scattered throughout the world acutely felt the need for a fresh lead, and this longing arose in them very strongly soon after the mystical event.

A most strange thing, almost like the dream, happened, however, while all these changes were unmistakably taking place in men's minds. With the advent of the quest, echoes of bygone events like the first faint rumble of an imminent earthquake seemed literally to be throbbing in the sky, so that those who were in the quest heard them distinctly, whilst the others who stood at a distance from them had an account of these echoes from the people of the quest. And as the echoes became gradually more and more audible one could even hear in them, if one were closely attentive, three distinct questions put from three distinct quarters of our habitable globe. They were questions addressed evidently to the spirits that guarded the cardinal secrets of the human race.

The questions were these.

If peace (*ananda*) has from immemorial times been set as the final goal of all creation, how is it that it is most unaccountably left to the mercy of *maya* (illusion) or to that which is changeful and unstable? If all creation can easily fall a victim to illusion what prevents truth or the *nirvana* from competing with illusion? If it is possible that man should lose himself to an outside force or agent, why is he not claimed by truth as its victim; or is it that man is too powerful for truth although easily pliable by illusion?

If God is love and peace is the final goal of all life how is it that love and peace are inscrutably left to the mercy of the Evil? If man can easily fall a victim to the demon, what prevents God from claiming man as his own victim? Or does God in His infinite mercy profess love for the demon as well, and will not choose between the demon and man?

If fiction is supposed to stand between man and his real self how is it that the real self does not stand between man and fiction? If man is overpowered by fiction what is there to prevent the real self from overpowering man? Or is it that the real self must not disown fiction if it owns man at all?

As the notes which spelt out the questions died down, leaving only an echo behind, what followed was the rise of a most anxious pleading for a reply. Curiously this pleading which seemed to come from all quarters of the globe was exactly the familiar comment on record which all the pilgrimages of history are known to have made with reference to the life that was set for man to live. The unseen spirits were told in no uncertain terms that the burden of life had been very, very heavy indeed and yet no replies ever came to the questions addressed to the spirits to relieve that burden.

Strangely enough, those who heard the questions and instantly recognized in them an echo of what had happened in their own personal history at some time or other, suddenly felt as if they had reverted to that history. They became metamorphosed into pilgrims and joined all the other pilgrims of history in pleading for a reply. In at least some tiny corner of our globe there was nothing but this pleading from one morning to another. It rose and fell in all the pitches of sound.

> The long ages laden with all the seasons on their devoted heads have passed the pilgrims by and yet the spirits still remain speechless and dumb. Will not the eternal spring ever come and melt the snows for good, so that the doors of the hermitage may open and will never shut again? It has been much too long, this anxious waiting. Have not the pilgrims with the load on their mind sat at the doors of the hermitage since immemorial times? How long still will the doors forget to open? Will they ever open? Even the stars on the horizon are greying with age and the earth is almost complaining that she has had to find food for the pilgrims from eon to eon.

Yet the climax was not reached till the pilgrims themselves began falling upon one another, perhaps for not knowing what they should do in the absence of any reply to their queries — "Why should not the doors open? What mysteries are being concocted behind the doors?"

And yet the issue which the pilgrims most humbly raised was not just an issue of struggle with life or of discipline. If they had gone through so much of discipline since history began they had had the courage that was requisite for it. Perhaps they found even a meaning in it and would not go without it. Even illusion, fiction and evil need not be too formidable for them if they are the only means by which they could have been given the chance of tasting suffering and discipline in life. They would on no account plead for a life which never once left the bed of roses. But it passed all their strength and courage to have to face illusion, evil and fiction, all three together and incessantly. Could even the universe which fills all space and all time find room enough for the courage which can face a perpetual clash between them? If the trial which this eternal clash produces promises no respite to the pilgrims, if its sole end is to make them go through the grind of only perpetual changes, what indeed could this trial possibly mean? **Or** has it no meaning but to be only a wanton purposeless enterprise on the part of the evil divinity?

Any pilgrim would willingly serve the hermitage in spite of the rigorous discipline it lays down, and the same may be said of the monastery or the city state which in other ways equally enjoin a hard and strenuous life. There is at least a certainty about them all and a purpose which one can easily read. But is it possible that one can serve the hermitage, the monastery and the city state all at the same time; and is it not a fact of history that the pilgrim is by force or persuasion called upon to serve them all? Is not that the meaning of history and of the perpetual warfare which it has embodied in consequence? Has there been any universe for the pilgrims where they could even after a lifelong service of discipline be in peaceful death for ever?

There has been no such universe for the pilgrims, and perhaps there has not been even a universe at all in the history that they have known. Instead there has been but one constant round of movement which illusion, fiction and evil by their perpetual clash produced. And such a movement had not even the pity to make room for the pilgrims to enjoy the respite of eternal death. If indeed there was any point in common between illusion, fiction and evil it was the emphatic claim that they all made to rule out extinction from the universe. To the hermitage as well as to the monastery and the city state extinction was a phantasy or a treason or a heresy. This was the primal message from them all and to this most cruel refusal to grant deliverance the sky, the earth and all the seas assented by their claim to eternal existence. There was no escape by the road to extinction, the whole universe proclaimed. The only prospect, then, for the pilgrims, it seemed, was to roll helplessly and roll for ever in the empty life-sucking vacuum — not even the respite of a sleep in eternal death.

In utter dismay and with some impatience they asked:

> Will this drama of illusion, evil and fiction then remain inscrutable for ever? Can we not have even the small mercy of knowing what theme is being enacted and how it is composed and what parts have been really allotted to us? If extinction is not the theme, if the hermitage, monastery and city state all equally spurn it, what is its theme and where exactly do we, the pilgrims, come in in that drama?

At this stage of most anxious pleading a Voice as if from nowhere began to speak:

> If history has been nothing but a drama of illusion, fiction and evil, as the pilgrims insist, there has been nothing in it that was wrong or strange, not to say hostile to them. It was indeed the only drama that could be enacted in the universe and the pilgrims were conceivably the only actors who had the privilege of playing on its stage. And the drama had to be played: there was no alternative and if ever the full perspective of this drama

> appears to them, a deep sigh of relief will come from the pilgrims themselves that nothing ever stood between the drama and them.

But this sounded like a conundrum to the pilgrims or a remote *ex cathedra* judgement; the pilgrims humbly wanted evidence and not a command to accept things as they were, cost them what it might.

The Voice changed its tone at once, as if it was not the same Voice that had just spoken. It spoke in stentorian tones:

> From where, please, does this right to ask for evidence arise? Who are the pilgrims, anyway, to ask for evidence or to claim the right to ask for it? They should know that rights go to those alone who can account for their primary capacity to exist and live. The rest are mere creatures who do not own rights but only opportunities by grace to live and fully enjoy what possibilities life can offer. Has there ever been any evidence that the pilgrims existed in an eternal time or had the right to decide whether to exist or not to exist? Can they now, when they seem to be so tired of life, even bring it to a close as they want to?

The Voice spoke with great impatience and the pilgrims heard to their bitter shame that they were mere creatures bound hand and foot by divine command and law. Their lot was cast in the meshes of illusion, fiction and evil and would never change till it was time for these mysterious agents to plunge back into the primeval chaos from whence they are called — perhaps, as a matter of choice.

The Voice spoke again:

> Is there again any clue in what the pilgrims call history, the only venue of life they know, as to the beginning and ending of things? If by all evidence they are glued to the present, which is equally remote from beginning and ending, could they possibly even receive answers to their questions, which

> must point to regions which no horizon of history has ever been able to hold? Why then ask questions? As creatures under divine grace or the beneficent law they should live the ideal life that has been set for them, and not ask questions or 'sulk' as children or young students do when they have to follow their mother's or teacher's steps.
>
> They must be grateful for the fact that they are still fully alive, sitting at the doors which guard the secrets, in spite of all that they have had to go through since the universe began. They should offer thanks to the Divine Spirit and the Law that the roaring cataracts have not drowned them a hundred times or the far-flung sky has not lifted them up *en masse* with both hands and cast them into the void of the surrounding chaos. They should pray and pray constantly that they may be given strength to bear up against the odds which illusion, fiction and evil perpetually throw in their way. It is not for the pilgrims to ask questions or to make complaints.

And why indeed should these complaints have been made when the whole course of this pilgrimage since it started one early, auspicious dawn, perhaps in some tiny hamlet at the remotest corner of the ever-expanding plain, had moved steadily upwards to reach a very remote and resplendent goal? Look at the distance travelled from that tiny hamlet and the almost endless time it had taken to cover it. The night was just receding and the sun waiting for the dawn to collect the last few shreds of the night. No sound was heard except the echoes from the hurried footsteps of the leopard retiring, or from the nightbirds circling back through the half-light to their leafy homes, or from the play of the wind like a flute in the bamboo groves since it left the mango orchards still bemoaning their loss, or from the watchdog warning the village that the barn was not quite safe yet from those who had to live by plying their trade at night.

And where is the sun in the heavens now and what time do the pilgrims make it? Where is that hamlet? Did they make their complaints when on that auspicious dawn they left the hamlet and did not they in that distant age see on the remote horizon a light and leave all they ever valued to reach it? Even the leopard did not go back to the woods that early dawn without a pang and the music in the bamboo groves was but an echo of what one could hear in the orchards. And yet the pilgrims had to leave the hamlet, since somehow they felt that life was a pilgrimage if it was anything. Its core was not in the hamlet but in their steady march towards the goal. The hamlet, whether it becomes an expanding village as the day arrives or a crowded city by the time the sun has reached the meridian, is but a stage which halts the pilgrimage, only to give it a shape in time. Where is all that faith gone? Why is it so madly replaced by scorching doubt? If life is a pilgrimage and the hamlet is but a halt in its course, can the pilgrims expect to live, if by a strange illusion they refuse to leave the hamlet and start on the pilgrimage again? The hamlet cannot hold them long, since it is but a stage of the pilgrimage. If the pilgrimage stops the hamlet will soon be claimed by the forest, or some avalanche of snow, or a deluge of rain from the mountains.

Yet why should they refuse to go out on the pilgrimage again? If what they call history, the record of all that they value, is but an account of the pilgrimage, what wonders were not lavishly displayed on its course? How the earth, with all her bountiful neighbours — the plains and the seas, the mountains and the forests — came out to bless them as they wended their way to the distant light! And each time the village or the city halted them, with bowed heads the people brought out their choicest specimens of art and craft for them to bless. And the whole countryside which came out to receive their blessings in festive robes greeted them with chants or spring blossoms in all shades and tones lying in their path. Was this all in vain or but the vainglory of the gossamer which only shimmers to match the shine of the sun? Or think of the light that steadily shines out from the mystical height: or the divine eminence wrapped in contemplative joy or in rhythmic movements which fills with glory every quarter of the globe: or the upstanding primal base of life on which stood God in eternal embrace with the universe? Do not these rare, unearthly lights give the pilgrims what they dearly love, their dignity, joy and assurance? Do not they treasure them as the final gift from the pilgrimage? Where else would they find them?

2

The Voice had suddenly stopped and at last the pilgrims making for the hermitage felt as if the doors of the hermitage were about to open. The spring was graciously riding the wind and all the rivers which ran incessantly down the innumerable heights brought a message from the snows that they had left the mountain tops this time for good. And as the pilgrimage started with the early morning sun the whole panorama of glistening heights in all conceivable proportions of elegance joyously opened wide. What splendours of green and white in masses of shapes and stature, and how they were worked in mosaics of myriad tints and tones: how again, this vast panorama was one whole piece of a movement in which an ever-bounding rhythm chose to work unseen!

It was midday before the pilgrims realized that they were almost back in the place they had started from. Did they count each step as they walked or were they just breathing the mountain air, or hearing the cataracts as they slipped down the heights, or watching the play between shadows and lights in the forest of trees? The flowers were yet to arrive but they could at least feel their presence in the anxious, expectant soil. But the birds were already wide awake and what calls they were sending out to their distant mates to come quickly and build up the nests!

"Was it then all a dream that we saw when the Voice spoke to us?" some of the pilgrims suddenly asked. "What was it all about?" Nobody could give an answer, as if they were in dream again. "Surely," some said, "we could not have strayed from the path to the hermitage. How could we, when even what we see and hear now may well be the hermitage or its gateway?"

They soon were of opinion that somehow they had been in a dream, the result of that very difficult climb before they had got to that hut the evening before. "That lap after a whole day's arduous journey broke us and we became fit only to serve as victims to dreams. What a dream indeed! Fancy, we came even to question the faith!" They prayed that they might never lose it again.

How long this spring lasted and how far the pilgrims climbed on their way to the hermitage is not known. There has never been a historical record of this pilgrimage. But the spring did not last longer than it had ever done and the snows certainly did not keep their promise. The winter arrived as usual. Sooner or later the whole of the mountain sides became a spotless white, even the cataracts became frozen with awe at the sight of that sudden panoramic change. The pilgrimage stopped for a long halt inside the ready-made wooden sheds waiting for them.

It was in the course of this long halt, when the pilgrims had had sufficient rest to regain their power of thought, that a most strange thing happened.

One night when they had all retired after a most brilliant day which played all the time with the snows around, suddenly a storm from the heights arose and everyone of the pilgrims heard suddenly nothing but voices which warned them screamingly of danger ahead. It was a pandemonium of sounds in which voices of many shades of tone and most diverse pitch struggled hard to raise a din. The pilgrims completely lost their balance. Were the voices those of the spirits of the mountain, which by long tradition never liked the pilgrims soiling their spiritual realm by their feeble human presence, or was it a revolt in the spirit world against the Voice which only the other day broke the pilgrims' resolve not to carry on with the pilgrimage till the replies to their queries had come? Some of the pilgrims in the din of sounds sat bolt upright in their beds, others seemed to be helplessly rolling down to the wooden floor, while the rest looked on with vacant eyes, clinging to their beds, all startled by fright. And if the storm had lasted very much longer they would have come out of their huts and started helter-skelter running down the mountainsides anyhow to reach the distant shadowy plains.

But the storm left as suddenly as it started and gradually the pilgrims came to themselves. And the first thing they did was to make a huge fire of logs and sit round it. It was now morning, fresh and crisp after the storm had gone, and the snow was glistening with pride again. They were still far from being in a decided state of mind but strangely enough by no means hopeless or altogether confused. They had, at least, one strong assurance and that was that they would sooner or later find out for themselves what it was all about.

At any rate, as some spoke out their minds, they were not going to be dupes of dreams or voices any longer. They would much rather take things into their own hands. Not that they were going to be foolish and stupid, and try to run their life unaided as if they were like gods who are credited with living as self-sufficient beings. At least as pilgrims they had to depend on aid to live from others, whether seen or unseen. But it did not follow that they must be equally dependent on external aids to know about things or even to find out the meaning of life; that they were not. Somehow that morning after the storm had gone they felt convinced that there was a difference between the art which is bound up with living and the science which caters for knowing. They were certain that they could find out what it was all about and they were determined that they would.

Exactly at this moment when their minds were made up about finding things out, the rebuke by the Voice that they were mere creatures came back to their minds. They did not, however, ask whether the Voice was at least as real a being as they themselves were. That question simply did not arise. Yet they could not dispose of that rebuke as an idle dream. They felt that they had to find out what exactly it meant and why it was delivered. Somehow the rebuke sounded like a challenge to them, and they were still by no means sure if they were not, as the Voice told them they were, mere creatures.

Gradually they also came to remember the queries which provoked the rebuke from the Voice. In fact, their whole past came back to them, and as they could not remember any answer to the queries from the Voice it fell in their estimation and looked like the Evil Incarnate of tradition, who plays on human weakness for his own end, either by open threat or artful cajolery. The Voice undoubtedly was astute enough but its astuteness lay in a very simple device, that of first stating a fact and then making a sheer phantasy look like fact by some strange manipulation of the original fact. The pilgrims frankly admitted to themselves that they were weak, but they were not going to be counters in the game of that Voice any longer. They would take things in their own hands and find out about them, unless the unforeseen happened again.

And the question that they all asked as they sat round the blazing fire was:

> Of what possible interest could it be to the Voice or to any other agent living to make of such a noble thing as the pilgrimage a mere tool in its hands or a counter in its games? How is it that illusion, fiction and evil are somehow let loose in the universe and the universe in consequence becomes only a stage for their sheer pranks? The pilgrimage no doubt started at the call of the light; it did start on an auspicious dawn from the hamlet in order to answer that

> call. But surely nobody knew or felt as it started that such a pilgrimage would soon be caught up in the meshes of illusion, fiction and evil. Why indeed should these denizens of darkness have come in to waylay its course? And if Light by all our hoary tradition had to rule them out eternally from its vast domain, who and what could have the courage to make room for them in their domain? What indeed are these denizens of darkness? Are they really dark or are they the agents of Light in disguise?

So the queries came back again in a more heightened form.

"It would be meaningless to argue," the pilgrims all said, "that they are instances of incarnate darkness and not just illusion or fiction, on the simple evidence that they are facts. Facts are facts and cannot be called by any other name, they say. But certainly even if we have to take them as facts and distinguish them from fancy we have still to account for their being. No fact ever succeeded by virtue of its strange habit of receding to an empty void in accounting for its being. The denizens of darkness will have to give at once other evidence to establish their claim to being. What could be that evidence, or is there no such evidence?"

The talk still continued and as it rose to a very high pitch indeed a log from the fire suddenly fell out with a terrific crackle. But even that extremely loud noise was drowned by the shout which came from some of the robust pilgrims round that fire.

> This is a very good omen indeed, we cannot possibly miss it now. It is a sure sign that the journey is almost at its end and we shall never have to stop again but shall be given the chance of going straight ahead till we stand face to face with the Light which started our pilgrimage. Oh! what a great moment it is for us!

Strangely, however, the rest of the pilgrims would not join in these shouts of joy but deliberately stood aloof.

We have no use for the omens and signs as you have; we have had enough of them. You may please yourselves. We will go entirely by what our own minds can offer us, however feeble they may be. We will stand on evidence which we can find or test for ourselves. We will, in a calm and collected way, go back to the queries and find an answer for them ourselves instead of waiting on omens and voices. It will be our special care indeed to answer the Voice which for its own hidden end demoralized the pilgrims. This may be impiety and sacrilege, but we stand by it.

3

Here began the age of Conference in the course of the pilgrimage, and the age of Voices steadily receded. A new epoch began in the history of pilgrimage. And if the queries certainly revived, they did not revive in the form of appeals to unseen gods and spirits. That phase seemed to have disappeared for good. Questions became instead problems and issues for the human mind to resolve, though those minds still continued walking the mountainsides as pilgrims. No voice for the moment was allowed to interrupt the proceedings in this pilgrimage, unless it was a voice that made "statements" and not a mere jumble of sounds, which may produce an enormous effect on the human mind but have no sense or meaning.

It is difficult to portray what exactly happened at this stage to the pilgrims, still intently moving on to reach the Light. They did not come back certainly to their normal state and start their search as normal human beings are expected to do. Perhaps they were half awake, or alternated between the state of metamorphosis and full waking life. They certainly were not pilgrims as they had been in the past. That was completely gone. They felt convinced that they were beings who could think out things. Yet they were still pilgrims and nothing but pilgrims. They were still too much under the influence of their immediate past and the life of pilgrimage to behave as normal members of states or seats of learning. The old path that the pilgrimage to the hermitage took was still the one they seemed to be travelling; only unlike their past selves they were treading the path as pilgrims of reason and not as pilgrims of faith. While they could not leave their old environment, the mountain path and its steady ascent to the hermitage, they as pilgrims became critical of the Voices and spirits which had led all pilgrims forward in the long past.

Certainly the state of metamorphosis in some form still continued but it cannot be claimed that the life of pilgrimage stood exactly where it was before. The fact was that as the pilgrims of faith gradually changed and became the pilgrims of reason the old pilgrimage came to an end and gave way to a totally new form. It was, however, still a pilgrimage and not a search. It was not time yet for the search to begin, since all those who were to carry it on were still, as it were, floating in the land of images. Only even in this land of images a very great change appeared. The new pilgrims did not continue merely to repeat their past but broke away from its usual path at a certain stage of it. In fact, the land of images in which the pilgrimage was taking place now was an altogether new pattern for the pilgrimage.

As we argue and reason in our dreams the pilgrims now argued and reasoned in the course of their pilgrimage instead of listening to Voices or praying for signs or appealing to spirits. And there was no reason why such a change in the course of the pilgrimage should not occur. The sphere of images, at any rate, is as real a sphere of existence as the sphere of sensations and percepts. In both spheres life in its complete structure appears and works out the same result. That is, at least, what some philosophers have been recently saying. The pilgrims of faith, therefore, are not more real figures than pilgrims of reason, and so the pilgrimage continued. The quest for the Truth which suddenly changed into this pilgrimage after the appearance in the air of the three queries was yet to become a search and cease to be a pilgrimage.

But the main theme in this new stage of the pilgrimage was to find a reason to meet the most poignant charge of the Voice that the pilgrims were, after all, creatures and had no will or mind of their own. Even as pilgrims it was not strange that they still should feel that their *locus standi* in the universe was not secure before the evidence for their status had been found. The hold of the Voice on the pilgrims was still fully operating. They could not quite deny that their freedom of action and thought somehow was liable to control, whether by the Lord of the universe or by what they called the denizens of darkness. And certainly it would be stupid for anybody to deny that they were not divine as they stood; some of the pilgrims simply shivered if such a claim even surreptitiously entered their heads. How then would they disprove the charge of the Voice that they were creatures; and if the charge stood, what was the point of holding a Conference to resolve the queries by thought, or any other technique which the pilgrims could construct? The alternatives were either to prove by indisputable evidence that the pilgrims were beings and not creatures, or to accept with humility what the Voice told them they had as a grant by grace from the Lord of the Universe. There was no third course.

Suddenly, however, at this stage some of the pilgrims felt inspired and seemed to see the exact answer to the question which the Voice had addressed to them. What they in a body were impelled to say was that a creature as such could never claim existence. That was the most absorbing assurance at the moment. And the reason for this sudden inspiration was that if there was a God who created the pilgrims as his creatures he had to exist in a pre-creating stage before that act of creation, or he would be perpetually creating his creatures. That would never do for him, as the God of all the universe had to be an absolute God and could not be subject to the limitation of any relationship. A related or relative God could not be absolute, as all tradition unanimously held. And perpetual creation, it was evident to these pilgrims, must imply that the God of the universe was bound to be only a related God if he was anything. But if God existed before his act of creation he would have to be the mystical God who certainly was eternally absolute and therefore capable of existing as the God of the universe. Divinity will not in such a situation stand to lose in any sense whatever. But the whole question of creation will at once go by the board, since the mystical God does not create and since absoluteness rules out creation for the simple reason that creation at once brings in the relative as a challenge to absoluteness. Those pilgrims who were talking under inspiration insisted on these grounds that there could not be creatures or creation, since God is absolute.

The argument seemed to make a great impression on the assembled company and even the logs sparkled to show their flaming assent. A few of the pilgrims, however, were not quite impressed. They thought that the logic of the case had by no means the right to ignore solid facts. The relative and changeful are facts which can legitimately demand recognition at least to the same extent as logic does. Better far then would it be to face the situation which between them the two are bound to create than to trust wholly either logic or fact. Here was, at least, a new situation and as the Conference was in no mood to take any dubious course, the suggestion of the minority was accepted, since at any rate it exploded the doctrine of creation and with it the charge that the pilgrims were mere creatures. It raised, no doubt, a fresh difficulty in the shape of the prospect of falling into a state of confusion. But that was not exactly a danger, however serious, which infected the pilgrims alone. The voice which so jubilantly brought the charge was equally liable to it, since all that is existent was liable to it except the

Lord of the universe, for whom the issue was quite different.

At any rate, there was no instance on record which testified to the fact that the Lord Himself made the charge. The charges were always made by those who claimed to be His agents and spoke in His name. And it made no difference what exact relationship with the Lord they all claimed for themselves. Perhaps if ever God had come down to earth Himself, he might easily have shown that illusion, fiction and evil were not as they had been taken to be, or if they did actually appear to be such and such, even that appearance itself had a meaning which was sure to unfold itself as the universe moved on. At any rate, the pilgrims did not confuse the agents or prophets with the Lord of the universe and were prepared to wait till God Himself had spoken. They were willing to believe that even His absoluteness, if God spoke about it, might well appear to be different from what has been associated with it. God might not claim to be absolute and illusion, evil and fiction might at once change their form. Whether this argument holds is another issue; but it held the pilgrims anyhow.

The pilgrims now were convinced that an alternative interpretation of both absoluteness and the three enigmas — illusion, fiction and evil — was possible. That was a clear achievement. But the conviction that such an interpretation could be formulated gave them the supreme confidence that they were not creatures; and it made no difference if they could not equally assure themselves at once what exactly their status in the universe was.

The pilgrims now unanimously decided that they would hold the next sitting of the Conference, and perhaps the last, where all pilgrimages from immemorial times came to close their round — that abode of the hermits which the mountains made on the banks of the lake specially reserved for the gods in the early dawn. How the waves in that lake sparkled like divine eloquence at the rapture of the forest all around when the blossoms and the full-throated songs of the birds met to herald the day! If the Voices still followed them they were trusted now to give advice and unravel issues which might fall beyond the pilgrims' reach. Since they had seen that they were not creatures but beings they could now trust any agent, seen or unseen. Even the Lord Himself might trust them now and help them in solving the issues which still remained unsolved.

It took the pilgrimage the whole of that summer to reach the hermitage on the lake of the gods. It was now autumn which made the forest drip with gold day and night except when the breeze picked up the earliest dew from its bed to moisten its grief for the departure of the summer green. It would soon be the time for the gossamer frost to arrive. The pilgrims settled down for a long Conference.

But before it was quite time for the Conference to begin in this last stage of the pilgrimage, the pilgrimage suddenly disappeared, like the blue showers from the sky which yield to the touch of the bright gold of the sun in the full tide of summer. Nothing of it survived. The whole of the mountain range and its hold on the pilgrims in all its seasonal moods lifted like a pall of mist from a valley. Not even the hermitage was there. The pilgrims were no longer pilgrims but stood in their city-spun garb anxiously debating as to the plan of the Search, except that they could not forget that somehow their debates about the Search had lost some of the threads with which it had at some time begun. As if by some sudden pressure on them they had had to drop the debate after it actually began, and had gone to sleep. And there was that vivid image of the hermitage upstanding; it was difficult indeed to believe that they had not been there. And some of the pilgrims at least openly held that the city, with all its arts, crafts and science, could not compare with the mountain range, nor that lake for the gods' morning bath, nor yet the play of seasons with the flowers and birds' songs in all the dales and valleys of the congregated heights. They affirmed that all this could not be mere dreamland or phantasy. It was a record which would gladden the heart of any historian, and not merely serve as a theme for the poet and perhaps the prophets as well.

But how was it that they had fallen into this dreamlike reverie? There were two things which distinctly stood out. They came out of it all with a firm conviction that they were not mere creatures, but beings who had a right to everything that is possible to an existent being. Besides, if they somehow were drawn into repeating a course of pilgrimage in the dreamlike reverie, they did not merely repeat the usual rhythm of it but definitely changed its movement at a certain stage. The part that was given to them to play as pilgrims of faith was changed by them into a part for the pilgrims of reason. Could one still call this sudden change into dreamlike reverie a mere phantasy?

Besides, they soon discovered that the Mystic himself who indicated the presence of the Truth went on his last pilgrimage at a very old age to that hermitage on the lake where their dream pilgrimage ended. Did it mean that the Mystic had his final grasp of Truth while he was in sight of Kailasa, as the Buddha had his illumination under the *bodhi* tree? What did it all mean? Was that hermitage, then, the symbol of peace that the Search for Truth was looking for, or perhaps what even the states in their Conference were unconsciously aiming at?

In this complicated state of mind the debating about the plan for a Search ended. It was now time for the Search to begin. If they were not quite satisfied with the plan one thing pleased them very much indeed, and that was that they knew the problems in the main which the Search had to resolve. And it was most peculiar that the problems should have been stated by the three questions which marked the beginning of their pilgrimage in a state of dreamlike reverie. Two things about this strange metamorphosis particularly struck them. It equipped them for the Search — no Search is possible unless one knows what the Search is about or, as the logicians say, the problem must be stated first before the solution can be seen. It gave them also full assurance that they were not mere creatures.

Part Three

The Search

1 The Search

The Search now began with full faith and assurance and the beacon that lighted its path was the declaration of the Mystic that the Truth was no longer cast in shadows but actually present in the world today. And its equipment was just a keen expectation that the questions that had for ages hung suspended in the air would now be resolved. And the men and women who began it were confident that they were in a position to receive and test any message that might be delivered. But they had no idea what the messages would be or of the possible sources from which they might come. They were still very much under the influence of the experiences which they had so recently had when they repeated the pilgrimage almost in the state of dream.

And yet it would be incorrect to call the Search people by the too familiar name of rationalists, although no rationalist or even the sceptic ever had so much self-assurance as they had. They knew exactly what the problems to be solved were and they had in addition the firm conviction that they could not be duped even by what are known as voices, signs or dreams.

Here indeed was a new type of man and woman in the history of the human race, who left every door open for the passage of light but never allowed any light to dazzle them. If the truth came from the image world, whatever its shape they let it come freely, but it had to give an account of itself if necessary. Even if the image world had to give way to some other realm which might choose to stand unknown, such an esoteric realm too would have to have its pedigree tested. While no phase of human experience hitherto known was preferred or discarded, none was allowed to override the supreme human test.

And one at least of the reasons why this group of men and women unanimously chose the Mystic as their beacon was that if he saw the Truth in a vision, he also indicated its actual presence in the world. What struck them most was that this great Mystic did not merely see a vision and offer it to the human race as such, as all the mystics had invariably done in the past. If he saw a vision as the mystics did, that vision referred to an actual presence which was open to observation by all. Obviously the issue of trust or authority with regard to the vision did not arise as it had done with every mystic vision in the past. What we may call confirmation by or consent from facts instead was firmly instituted in its place. If the Mystic saw a vision, the Truth that he saw in that vision referred to an actual, historical fact which could be easily verified.

Perhaps it is a question if ever there was such a vision in the records of any tradition. The visions of history pointed to divinity, or the core of reality, or some eternal principle. They stood as witnesses of the Divine, or the Absolute, or the timeless Reality. As visions they were just media through which the Eternal was believed to approach the Temporal, so distant and remote from it. Even when the claim was made that the historical came actually to hold the Divine as a result of that approach, the historical Divine was not identified with the mystical Divine but described as the Son of God. And yet even this unusual division in the nature of Divinity would not have mattered if it had already been historically known who the Son of God was or might possibly be. The mystical claim that God sent His Son to earth had to be taken on trust or authority and this authority again was not God's direct commandment. It was expressed through an agent, call him by whatever name you like. The agent was not God Himself. Even when the Son of God declared himself that his Father was in Heaven, he was called upon to prove that he really was the Son of God. And the moment the issue of proof arose, authority lapsed unless it was preserved by force.

If, indeed, there was history, it was a standing evidence that the Divine was not there or why should there be history at all? There could not in the nature of things be any trace of divinity in it and so no mortal could possibly have had the chance of knowing who the Divine really was or what exactly He was or could be like. In any case, the Son of God could not be recognized even if he put on human garb as a mark of goodwill to the human race. All that would be recognized in him was bound to be the human garb. He may at the most appear as the perfect man, but even that only to some and not certainly to all.

All visions in the past, therefore, had to depend on authority or trust, and so consent from facts or confirmation by evidence could be recognized as the test. And after this the somewhat spurious claim on their behalf that they brought peace and resolved doubt in human history stood equally contradicted in that same history. Even at this late hour the issue is not how to consolidate peace and faith, but how exactly to trace their sources. In any case a good portion of the human species stands today in an extremely destituted state, as at least a part of it always has done.

It is another issue what view the Mystic himself held about the Eternal or the Absolute. He was a mystic of long, mature years. He was a *yogi* who did the pilgrimage year in and year out and ministered to the needs of society with great compassion. It was inconceivable that he would pass over the *atman* or *nirvana* in his long pursuit of Reality, since he was born and bred in the mystical school. But somehow he did not refer to the *atman* or *nirvana* as tradition has known them when he indicated the presence of Truth in human history. It is quite another question why he did not refer to his ancestral wisdom as it was formulated in the Scriptures, even though his whole life was but one continuous effort to work out the authority of those Scriptures. Perhaps he saw more than was seen by his predecessors; perhaps to him the Scriptures stood in a different light, easier to grasp and nearer to fulfilment. All these questions cannot be answered now.

But he was a *yogi* and what he said had its origin in yogic insight. The place indicated for Truth appeared to him in a vision. It was not the result of observation or rational thinking or even a gift from some Spirit who may be ruling our Universe. At any rate, no further information is available about him, as he is gone from this earth.

It may sound strange, but it is equally true that there is no historical record of the men and women who were in the Search as it began. It is impossible to state their numerical strength or the place from which they started or the destination to which they were bound, or finally, the cultures and civilizations from which they came. The Search, however, was a historical fact and not an occult or even dream experience. Some day, perhaps, the historian will trace it. In the meantime one may with perfect reason describe it as just a society or community of men and women; and that description ought to be enough for us in our attempt to follow the successive stages through which it ran and trace what its final achievement was as a result of them.

But one can with perfect reason argue that at least some of the people who initiated the Search must have come from the people of Asia, known as the Group people. The evidence for this simply is that the Search was led by the declaration of the Mystic as its beacon. One cannot argue about the presence of the non-Group people in this Search in exactly the same way. The individualist of the twentieth century, however sceptical, does not respond to the mystic as the Group or the caste people naturally do. Even the people who stand between the individualist and the Group people may also not respond to a mystic. After all, mysticism was a heresy in the Church which these people followed.

It is simply not true, however, that the Search was constituted by the Group people alone. The truth is that all the civilizations existing today were equally represented in this Search as it began. It is another matter how they happened to come together or why. That is for the historian to trace.

But no man or woman after they joined the Search, whatever their ancestry, professed any faith other than what the Search distinctly laid down. They were in consequence all out in quest of Truth, which in their view no civilization had ever found. And so they belonged now to a new scheme of society, even if it was still very immature and unformed.

All this need not imply that they all came right out of their different ancestries or the societies in which they were born and bred, as if they could no longer be in any sense subject to any of the habits of thought, feeling and action which their ancestries had built up as techniques of living in the course of ages. A clean departure from tradition was not possible and that for two clear reasons.

The society they formed to pursue the Truth as indicated by the Mystic had no provision for all their needs as human beings. It did not cater for their subsistence or defence, or even a resolution of the conflicts that they might still be heir to for the simple reason that they had come from different stocks with even conflicting interests.

The other reason was that there was no ancestry which did not believe in the final achievement of absolute peace and truth. Even if none of them accepted the view of truth and peace which the others held, they all agreed that Truth and Peace were the real goal. Perhaps, side by side with their profession of truth and peace there had been an undercurrent of feeling in them that the real Truth and Peace were still as far distant as ever.

It is perfectly arguable that they never left the range of their ancestral homes nor lost their attachment to them. For at least subsistence and defence they had to seek the aid of society and in addition to their dependence on it they had the inward conviction that the final achievement of Truth as the Mystic indicated would also embody the fulfilment of all ancestries.

The constitution of this new society, therefore, in its initial stage was bound to be very simple indeed. It had all the appearance of just a pilgrimage and differed from the pilgrimages of the past only in the sense that it had no faith in any notion of reality which still held the old traditions together. The destination for this new pilgrimage was not Kailash or Jerusalem or the Parthenon. Perhaps it was not quite known what the destination was. Only one thing counted for these new pilgrims and that was the Mystic's indication. There was nothing else to go by except what it pointed to as a historic event in the form of thought. They certainly were not familiar with that thought but had the full conviction that it would be found. How it will be found and where is another issue. There is no fixed abode for thought and even if an abode is built for it in the shape of a book, the book may fail to hold it except to a very few and maybe only to one. The object of the Search, therefore, is by no means easy to describe, but its existence is unquestionably a historical fact.

Such a pilgrimage can have in the nature of things no constitution. If it depends for its defence and subsistence on the existing societies which aim at realizing the ideals of old it will have the proportions only of an esoteric group or an exclusive society within it like the groups known as artistic, philosophic or scientific. As such, since it will in the nature of things be perfectly harmonious and single-minded, it will not need a constitution, the need for which does not normally arise unless there are factors which do not coalesce. Besides, by its detachment from all other bodies except when it halts in its search for food or shelter or suddenly reverts to a traditional mood, it will be exempt from the need of building a constitution to meet the challenge from other bodies arising from differences with them. Exactly the same reason which accounts for the absence of a constitution will account for the absence of a code of conduct for the individuals who constitute it. A harmonious body which acts spontaneously does not need such a code. All such pilgrimage, as long as it lasts, is just a steady flow of harmony and leaves behind it only a deposit of deeds. No code of conduct is needed for it. The code generally arises when the pilgrimage comes to an end and the *mandir,* the church or the temple is built in its place. By that time, the sun must be blazing hot on the horizon and the pilgrims are recalled hastily from their well-earned rest to stage a facsimile of the pilgrimage again. Arguments soon prevail and the claim for Truth needs even force or persuasion to establish it. We enter here the region of constitution and code as known in history. What the result of all this in the end has been in all tradition we need not repeat. No light in this region ever shone except in a penumbra of darkness and no darkness ever remained only dark. Perhaps there has been nothing which was light or darkness, but only illusions of them. No constitution produced any phase of the result that was intended.

2

The Search now was on the open road and just completing the first stage of its arduous journey when a very strange thing happened. They came into touch with various groups of men, women and children who seemed to be aimlessly wandering about as people do very often outside the Western world. To all appearance they had no fixed abode and perhaps no fixed destination to go to. All their belongings they carried on their heads or in ramshackle transports most of which were improvized. How woebegone and destitute they looked!

It soon became apparent that these groups of men and women must be the straggling remnants of whole civilizations in retreat. There had been millions recently who began such a retreat when all that they had ever valued or possessed went up in smoke with countless villages, towns and cities. No trace of them can be found on this earth today unless we take the rumblings that preceded the recent earthquakes as their groans. Why such conflagrations should appear as a result of sheer human dread or pride rather than of the periodic impatience of the elemental world is perhaps the most difficult thing to see; and the long puzzle of human history has been that these are just the occasions when the serene and thoughtful in the human family should have felt assured that peace had arrived on earth. This puzzle becomes an enigma when the sky as it soon lights up with the flaming anguish of soul also resounds with shouts of joy and triumph to match that conflagration in its attempt to touch the roof of the sky. The historian, with quaint humour, recorded that what went up in smoke was the primeval darkness, while the shouts of triumph were only divine blessings which the gods carried down from on high to the victors on earth. The story is repeating itself almost daily in the twentieth century, and it seems there is no ground for hope that it will not repeat itself as time advances.

That at any rate was exactly the feeling in the minds of the men and women in the Search when they came into touch with these aimlessly wandering groups of men, women and children. Even the forest is benign to its denizens compared to what human society has given as status to these wandering millions of all ages. Will the earth ever be secure for man? The Search almost began to repeat what as pilgrims they had pleaded.

The immediate call on the Search, however, was to provide both food and shelter for these destitute wanderers. And soon, very soon, the men and women in the Search went out in a body to collect what they could find in the neighbourhood to meet their immediate needs. The Search, in consequence, seemed to fall into abeyance or perhaps a portion of the journey for the Truth meant ministering to the needs of fellow men and women when they were completely destitute and in pain.

In about a couple of months or so, they were fortunate enough to provide for a good many of the helpless and to find work for some with the help of the neighbourhood. This brought a sense of great relief: but what really filled them with joy and gratitude was that a good few of the wandering people should actually have joined them in the Search. These men and women, among whom were great historians, philosophers and even noted divines, were greatly struck by the extremely simple and open faith of the people in the Search and especially by the way in which they lived in perfect peace and harmony. Indeed the Search brought back to their minds the record of all great movements of history when they began. Yet they could not but notice that while the people in the Search chose to live a life which was simple and pure they were also fully self-assured and conceded to all the same freedom and independence as they knew themselves. There was humility in them but not at the expense of their freedom, a sense of uniqueness and personality but not to the detriment of their unity. And although the constitution of the society they had formed had yet to develop any clear outline, the learned scholars felt that when developed it would be neither hierarchic nor democratic. Besides the Search people did not preach to them or even tell them about what their ideal or objective was. It was they who found out about the Search by asking questions. What could be the secret of the life of this Search which was so strange?

Some of the scholars, however, had clear misgivings and wanted more than the others to go deeper into the implications of this Search. How could any group of people, whatever their goal or faith, preserve both the values: unity and individuality? How was it possible to avoid both hierarchy and equality in any organization? Perhaps the people in the Search did not know what pitfalls were waiting for them ahead; perhaps they were naïve in their faith or had been under the spell of some racial myth or scholastic jugglery, or complicated sophistry, or just a mere desire to cut the Gordian knot by an act of plain detachment from life.

Soon there was a division of opinion among the historians, philosophers and divines. Some wanted to take the Search people as they appeared to be. And if that might not be altogether wise, could it mean any consequences worse than what all civilizations had invariably made the human species suffer? Besides, there was at least some chance in such a procedure of escaping the fate which the wisdom of all the ages never failed to bring them to. The others wanted not to leave the path that was known and familiar, however difficult it might have been. "Perhaps the future, if we follow this Search without any assurance, may take us to the very den of the Demon, which certainly we have escaped so far. No tradition was quite pitch dark; there was, at least, some glimmering of light if only to indicate the path ahead in darkness."

So the second stage of the Search did not begin as the first did in a state of perfect oneness of spirit. Even the Search people themselves felt that perhaps they had not quite reconnoitred the ground before they set out on their journey. If they were now called upon by the newcomers to answer questions as to the bona fides of their search, they were like the pilgrims who called upon the Spirit to enlighten their minds. Surely there was nothing unnatural in all this. If the Search gave the newcomers the impression that it stood on a basis which was never known in history, they had to ask questions about that basis. Perhaps it is only such an enquiry from others outside the Search that could lead to the formulation of the nature of that basis. And certainly such an enquiry could not do any harm to that basis or to the prospects of the Search. It was inconceivable that the Search would lose its faith in its beacon even though it might fail to answer at once the questions which the scholars and the divines most naturally raised. Nor was it a fact that the Search had no questions of its own to answer. Indeed, the Search was planned to reach the destination of Truth only so that the eternal questions of all pilgrimage might be solved. Perhaps the questions of the scholars, historians and divines at bottom meant in a different form those very questions which the pilgrims had raised. The scholars and divines might well be pilgrims in disguise.

At this moment, when the journey for that day was nearing its end, some people from a neighbouring village came up to the Search with an invitation to them to spend a couple of days in a large mansion almost on the edge of a famous lake. It was a very ancient building and report has it that it had made a home at different times for Royalties and Jesuits. The beautiful lake was held in rapture as it were in the outstretched palms of two rows of wooded mountains facing each other, chanting hymns to God in the Heavens night and day. The news about the Search had already spread to the countryside and the whole atmosphere was full of fresh light rising from the sun that dispelled the surrounding mist.

There is a saying in the neighbourhood that the first night the Search spent in this ancient dwelling on the lake either there was a severe storm which swelled the lake into an unusual fury or a violent debate took place between the Royalties and the Jesuits as to what could be the meaning of this Search. Why should their well-deserved peace of centuries be disturbed by these strange renegades from the traditional path? "What has happened to the state," the Royalties asked, "that we left behind well-armed and strong", "And how does the Church fare today," the Jesuits most politely enquired, "that we spared no pains to consolidate on earth?"

The village did not sleep either that night, but the Search had no sense of that debate. To all in the Search the whole night seemed to be pouring out chants and hymns, except to the few divines who could not believe that it was all straightforward and clear. There was something still hanging about, they felt, which might mean even death to all that they ever professed.

And as the day broke with the mountains broadening on all sides either on flat pasture lands or on steadily-rising, billowy woods on a granite base the village greeted the Search, almost flaming in the gold of the pine. There was not a chalet which had not the blessing from the neighbouring pine.

Rumour has it that the forest on the mountains moved down the heights one day to lend its aid to the architect to mould his structural frame. And once that happened the architect never lost the feel of that embrace of the forest. It was an issue after that event where indeed the pine of the forest was.

The Search had its morning meal on the simple fare that the village prepared for them. And then talk began. They chose a retreat in the mountains for this talk within easy distance of the lake.

The issue was raised by a minister of the Christian church who was supported by a historian of the secular school.

The minister claimed that there really was no need or occasion for the Search since the Truth was finally revealed 2,000 years ago.

> God sent His only Son to the earth. Here is an evidence of Truth based on fact which even the simplest folk could easily grasp. Who did or can ever miss this Truth when it stands out in the garb of a fact? It is the fact which is the direct and immediate experience of man, the primal base of his life. Was not the Son of God born? Did He not preach the Truth and proclaim that His father was in Heaven? And what happened to Him as a result of that preaching of the Truth? Can human history ever forget His death on the Cross?

This was what the Christian Divine with great emphasis put forward.

The historian followed him to make a case for fact as such. "Human experience," he said, "unless it is consistent and can be tested by verified facts is but illusion or fiction. If the Search, on its own showing, has pinned its expectation of Truth to a mere mystic vision, it cannot possibly have a basis which will stand any valid test. One has to go by what is attested by historical evidence and not by what may be called a peculiar grasp by the mind of the unverifiable or the meaningless." It sounded as if the professor in the laboratory was speaking again.

There was no reply to these claims from the men and women of the Search. But another historian spoke up rather sharply and he was followed by the most noted philosopher of the groups who had joined the Search on the first day of the journey.

> It is too late in the day to make a case for the birth of the Son of God, and the reason simply is that nobody ever has known what divinity is or what a Son of God could possibly be. If God truly existed on earth, perhaps like us mortals he too might have had a son. But no experience of history, which certainly deals with verifiable facts as much as illusions and fictions, ever contained the Divine or the son of the Divine as beings existing in it. There was no such fact. There was a lot of loose talk about Divinity, no doubt, but such talk led to flat contradictions leaving no experience behind in the end. What, then, is meant by saying that the Son of God was born, or that God saw to it that the Son of God should be born 2,000 years ago and not a day earlier or later?

At this rate, the oft-repeated claim that the mathematician actually saw the "round square" coming up one morning to shake hands with him would also be sound.

"The difficulties," the second historian pointed out, "are two: the terms 'divine' and 'son of God' are meaningless. So there is no conception of these terms which can appear in a statement or proposition. And could a meaningless term be verified by a fact of experience? If we cannot know what divinity means as a historical entity, could we see the actual God Divine? It is another matter," the historian further added, "whether human history ever recorded the Christian claim — history is full of such claims. But no historian would call 'facts' by the name of tales and all claims about Christianity are but tales. And if this deficiency is to be retrieved by a fresh claim that Christianity has been professed by millions for whom it was the only source of comfort and peace, such a claim again can be easily challenged by the fact that it equally brought misery and anguish of soul to many millions by the way it rode roughshod over their beliefs and faiths. Finally, even the Christians themselves had to pay for what Christianity guaranteed to their own forbears. It is recorded history that what one generation achieves in the way of success, peace and joy, another generation has to pay for; and the reason is that no success ever is achieved except at the supreme expense of some failure somewhere. And those who fail because others must succeed invariably make the posterity of the successful pay. If, therefore, the history of Christianity is a fact, it does not mean that Divinity is also a fact or that God's son was actually seen on earth, not to talk about his establishing a Kingdom of Love. Here was a history of tales and not facts, though the tale itself was a fact."

The philosopher now followed and to the astonishment of all made an exceptionally strong case against both the minister of the church and the two historians. And incidentally he did not spare the mystical claim as it lay in its traditional form. Perhaps he had reached almost the level of scepticism before he came across the men and women in the Search. At any rate, to him history was actually reduced to smoke in the latest conflagration which the human race had just been through. Nothing remained over except the bare hope that a change might by some miracle be coming soon.

He very quietly offered to the whole gathering what he called a résumé of history, and in it he made the impressive case that history so far has been nothing but a vast panorama in which three definite civilizations with three distinct objectives or ideals periodically clashed with one another, the total result being always a conflagration. Perhaps this view was not altogether familiar to all minds and there might have to be a few more conflagrations to bring it home to some: but there can be no escape from it. It is impossible that the claim for any of the three civilizations can be made to prevail. The perpetual failure for ages has made that necessity abundantly clear.

The philosopher was not a hardened sceptic by any chance but he had no use for the mystic or the dualist or the humanist who had hitherto alternately prevailed in human history. What he pointed out with great firmness was that not one of them had succeeded in even proving that there was a universe, not to speak of actually establishing it for good.

> There have been, instead, three conceptions of the universe in a state of perpetual clash. The whole of the objective reality that they stood for was exhausted by the time the claims for it, by virtue of their incompatibility, ended in confusion. Indeed there was no objective reality other than these conflicting claims, if we go by history: so that we cannot choose between a drama which enacts tragedy and comedy in turn with the fifth act played on an empty stage, and history which embodies all the objective world in the shape of an alternate rise and fall of conceptions ending in confusion. There has been a series of forms of each conception, no doubt, but as the final stage each time marked nothing but confusion even the historian of each series could not survive to hand over his records to the historian of the next stage.
>
> Where, then, is the historian? What fact does he put on record if it is not the immediate present; and do we make a record of an event if we are in the event; and if we are not in the event, what record do we make of it unless we call it phantasy? All this may sound like sophistry or sheer dialectic. But the conflagration from which we have just escaped with our body and perhaps a little of our soul was not sophistry or a mere dialectic."

3

The philosopher then proceeded to describe in greater detail the three civilizations of history. By this time the minister of the church was getting restive but the mountains made a gesture with their tall, straight pines bending to the winds which had just arrived to catch the sense of the point the philosopher was making. Or perhaps they wanted to broadcast the philosopher's speech.

The philosopher claimed that the Hindu, the Jew and the Greek as types stood out in what we call history for all time, forming three distinct social schemes which never constituted a unity except when confusion or conflagration inevitably arose.

> The universe, then, was nothing but this confusion: and it followed that both the historian and the dramatist were drowned in it and nobody heard the divines pray any longer. But in the periods when the Hindu, the Jew or the Greek either stood erect and made claims or suffered from the demise of those claims they appeared in all spheres of life as direct opposites. As individuals they formed three distinct types of individuality, and equally, the societies they formed were three distinct societies.

Finally the objectives and the technique of realizing them which they professed were also three. (Perhaps the still-surviving Pythagorean would find in the number — three — some cosmic significance!) But the total result of this strange fact that there were three types of individuals, societies and objectives as the sole constituents of the universe was that there was only a universe of clash with no background to uphold them. If the Greek as an individualist emphasized individuality, he could not possibly agree with the Hindu who spurned individuality and emphasized unity. And both of them were sure to disagree with the Jew or the Christian who spurned both individuality and unity and emphasized community. And so, necessarily, the caste of the Hindu, the class of the Greek and the community of the Jew or the Christian clashed. In exactly the same way, unity, individuality and relationship which they respectively espoused as ideal objectives could not but come into conflict.

"My conclusion," the philosopher said, "is that none of them at this late hour could with any reason bring forward any known historic plea as a challenge to this Search, provided that the Search is not merely a repetition of some old mystical urge. But as I, for one, have felt that it is not a mere revival of mysticism but an altogether fresh view I am prepared to follow it till, at least, the crucial moment for testing it has arrived. If none of the ancient, medieval or modern modes of thinking and acting are surviving today, it is odd that we should be bringing up again their effete and worn-out claims as a challenge to this Search. The outstanding fact of the situation is that the Search has made no claim on its own behalf, not to talk of persuading wanderers to join them nor has it in any way interfered with the existing societies. And if they are not leading a completely detached life, at least they never even call on the villages or towns or cities for help as they pass through them, unless they can give a return in some form of service. The Search has worked its way with services to the communities for whatever help they have received. And it is a fact that they have offered help to them for the sheer joy of helping them. What is the point of preaching to such a body at this late hour the story of the Gospels or the myths of the scientist or the well-known antinomies of the scientific or philosophic speculations? Besides, if it is a fact that the Search has, at least, impressed us all as an unusual group which somehow managed to avoid both the autocratic and the democratic, could we not for the sake of experiment give them a chance to prove our expectations?"

It was time to close the meeting, as the villagers were anxiously expecting them to come to their midday meal. The sun had just come out of a bank of cloud and the cattle in the pastures suddenly looked up to see what was really happening in the sky. There was a great gathering on the lakeside in front of the building when the Search came down from the mountains to have their midday meal. They had their meal served inside this building while the whole village turned up to have theirs just outside on the promenade so beautifully sheltered. And yet what festival it was, whether it was Pagan or Christian, it would indeed be difficult to say. At any rate, some of the men and women in the Search who did not come from the European stock attracted the greatest attention, especially of the women and children of the village. Report has it that the sadness that like a pall of mist had been hanging over the whole village for some time was for the moment gone; even the cattle in the neighbouring pastures in unison with the pine-clad mountains persuaded the lake to splash about in one of its famous rhythmic movements in ripples of all colours, which the sun watched from the sky and filled graciously with his steady golden beams.

The meal was over; and the whole village followed the Search to their mountain retreat and sat in a circle round them to listen to the talk which soon began again. The gold was still streaming down from the sun and the village below with the cattle in the pastures stood wrapped in silence, so that it too might catch the swing of the long arguments that the Search developed.

The talk was begun by the people of the Search, who put before the scholars, historians and divines a view which had struck them. This view had to do with the résumé of history which the philosopher had presented to the assembly in the morning session.

> If history has been nothing but a conflict of objectives, since these were held by three distinct civilizations in a relation of perpetual opposition, does it not follow that the objectives must be illusions and not truths? Could one possibly conceive of a clash between truths, or even between truths and illusions or falsehoods? How again could objectives clash as they do unless those who uphold them have put all their energy into efforts to realize them? It seems to be elementary that inasmuch as the Hindu, the Christian and the Greek organized their life with the sole purpose of realizing the ideals of unity, individuality and community, history at once became a record of warfare. And the final episode has to be conflagration. There is nothing in history but a clash of efforts to realize illusions. Not one of the groups who have joined us need forget so soon what conflagration is and how it may still be pursuing them.

The philosopher was perfectly justified in reminding us that there have been three theories on every issue whether it touched divinity or humanity, facts or ideas, the verifiable or the transcendental. Indeed the Search would not have come into existence at all if there had been any reply to the outstanding problems of history anywhere. And the Search indeed has been in existence ever since the sky blazed forth with the first instance of conflagration.

What had especially struck the people in the Search was that the philosopher's résumé completed the analysis of history so definitely begun in the dream and continued in the quest. If the quest painted the negative features by referring to the frustration of all purpose on account of the enigmatic presence of illusion, fiction and evil, the résumé pointed out that the purposes themselves were equally illusory. The conclusion of this wholesale repudiation of history was that none of the three civilizations succeeded in preserving any of the values which were in conflict: unity, individuality and community.

"Does it not follow, then," they asked, "that the whole experiment of human civilization to preserve one or other of the three values — unity, individuality and community — by staging a wholesale conflict between them has completely failed? How could the device of valuation possibly succeed in the teeth of impossibility of choice and of selection of conflict as the technique for realizing that device? The fact is that the long experiment did not even end in a situation in which one side prevailed while the other went down for good: it passed, inexorably, through two stages of contradiction, followed by a third in the shape of complete confusion and contrariety. Perhaps the only streak of light on the horizon today is that it seems to be no longer possible to repeat that experiment."

This comment by the Search people on the résumé of history simply gripped the meeting. And the question the bulk of the members asked was:

> Should we then carry on making efforts to realize our objectives if we have to accept them all as illusory? Would there be any point in making such efforts? Could we not on the contrary practise abstention instead with regard to those objectives? If all attempts, however earnest, to realize them have invariably resulted in frustration, how could we still make fresh conscientious efforts to realize the objectives? Besides, it should not be difficult for us to change the course of our action altogether by deliberately practising restraint whenever, as a matter of habit, we may feel an urge to try to realize them?

The people of the Search were in complete agreement with this plea for abstention and restraint. In fact, according to them there was no other alternative if the path of reason was followed. They added:

> An end or objective is amenable to both types of activity — we can act to realize it or act to abstain from realizing it. There is plenty of evidence in all tradition as to what restraint or abstention means and no civilization forgot to sanction it as the only legitimate procedure when the occasion for dealing with fiction, illusion or the evil arose. Why then should we not start practising abstention with regard to all the objectives if we have to accept them as illusions? Why should not the Hindu, the Christian and the Greek equally abstain when their values of unity, community and individuality are in deadly and open conflict?

At this stage of the talk both the minister of religion and the historian of the modern school in almost frantic protest held up their hands. They unmistakably felt as if the ancient Asiatic practice of self-immolation was being quietly revived by the Search without recognizing the prospect of the complete extinction of the human species which it involved. They said with great emotion:

> Certainly abstention if it is practised by the human race would be a dire misfortune and not by any means an improvement on what the conflict of civilizations has so far yielded. History, the venue of all conflict, has at any rate been a record of survival if nothing else, even if it has staged periodic conflagrations. Besides, there is no evidence that it will write off that record and stage complete extinction in its place. To put wholesale abstention in its place is to invoke the evil of voluntary suicide — a prospect which could have an appeal to an absolute sceptic but to no other creature on earth. It is the most ungodly theory

ever contemplated and perhaps, evil incarnate.

This challenge came from a deep-rooted instinct in human history, and soon provoked a sharp reply from the philosopher, at once simple and direct.

"In my opinion," the philosopher quickly said, "the theory of mutual abstention has nothing whatever to do with ungodliness; and the case for it stands on indisputable grounds. If the objectives to be abstained from are without any doubt illusory they cannot possibly be made the goal of realization. And if hitherto we have made deliberate efforts to realize them we have done so on the ground that we believed them to be true. It would be senseless to suggest that we can still continue making such efforts even when we are convinced that they are wholly illusory. It would be strange if we distinguished between truth and illusion as opposites and at the same time reacted to them as if they were identical. The point, therefore, which has been made by the people of the Search, that we cannot but abstain from our objectives since we are convinced that they are illusory, stands. We cannot go back to warfare and its consequences, the periodic conflagration, simply because the bare logical implication of the method of wholesale abstention may look to some like immolation of our species."

At this point the people of the Search again intervened to elucidate the main points at issue. They dissociated themselves completely from any idea of self-immolation and steadily affirmed that it was a mistake to think that the Hindus or any other Asian people, any more than the Greeks or the Christians ever held such a theory. The truth about the Hindus is that they wanted, unlike any other people, to reach the level of the Real, which existed according to them outside the illusory world, and to attain Absolute Bliss in full consciousness. The issue, however, is not what the Hindus did or did not believe; the issue is whether the theory of abstention necessarily implies in practice complete extinction.

And here, as a preliminary to a solution of that issue, they made reference to the nature of conflict as such, which to them was really at the back of all human problems.

> It would be stupid to suggest that we have got into all this trouble simply because we wanted unity, community or individuality as our ideals. There is perhaps nothing wrong with them as such and one may even add that we shall in all probability never come across any fresh ideal which will contradict them. But, unfortunately, it so happened that those ideals never could escape conflict and it is exactly this strange intervention of conflict which was the source of all our trouble. The issue for us is to trace the origin and meaning of this conflict.

The people of the Search were very modest as they proceeded to analyse the nature of conflict. They laid no claim to scholarship and did not pose as historians or philosophers. They were speaking as men and women of common sense who by sheer good fortune had had the chance to lay in a store of real experience. They descended from ancient races and they had in their blood the deposit of long acquaintance with varied faiths and cultures. The point they made about conflict referred to the necessity of a background to it.

> It is really the keynote of the whole history of conflict except in its ultimate form. If a conflict means a relation of disagreement between two opposite groups it also means a background of agreement between them with regard to some ideal or objective. If, indeed, there happened to be no such common meeting-ground the groups upholding the values could not possibly have clashed. The values in clash are but functions on the part of those groups to realize the

> common objective; and they clash simply because there are two opposite ways of realizing that common objective.

The theory evidently was original and even unusual and so there was a general expectation that it should be illustrated if possible. And here the Search people referred to the philosopher, who alone was capable of citing illustrations from the recorded history of two major civilizations — the Hindu and the Greek. "Have you not," they asked, "come across evidence in that history which will confirm our theory of conflict?"

The reply of the philsopher was short and precise; it made only two points which accounted for the theory and defined the nature of the community in which conflicts arise.

"My thesis," the philosopher said, "is that conflict never takes place except in a group or community and the community has always two spheres of activity — one in which the common interest is worked out on behalf of the whole community, with no party division or clash; another in which the interest that is to be worked out is no longer common but dual. In fact, there are two conflicting interests here and the community stands divided in this sphere into two sections as either contradictories or contraries."

> It should be possible for anybody to verify this view of community and conflict from his or her own experience whatever his or her station in life may be. And if we still want evidence from historic records we shall easily find it in the well-known conflict between the Brahmin and the Buddhist in Hindu history or that between the Platonist and the Atomist in Greek history. If it is a fact that both the Brahmin and the Buddhist professed unity as their goal, they certainly also clashed on the plane of the realization of that goal. And the same is true of the Platonist and the Atomist, who accepted individuality as their goal and then came into clash as they proceeded to realize it, the two

> incompatible modes of reaching the goal — autocracy and democracy — being responsible for the difference between them.

This interpretation of the implications of conflict and their verification produced great satisfaction and some of the gathering called upon the philosopher to add to his analysis by pointing out where the exception to this general feature of conflict appeared, which gave him the chance of defining the nature of conflict in its ultimate proportions.

The philosopher held that there was one exception to the co-existence of agreement and disagreement in all cases of conflict and this exception appeared when the three ultimate civilizations of history clashed with one another.

"These organizations," he said, "are the mystical or group civilization, the humanistic or class civilization and the dualistic or community civilization."

> There has been, in my opinion, no record of a common background in the conflict which has through all history raged between these three civilizations. No historian has so far testified to its presence perhaps because no philosopher ever propounded a theory about the origin of those civilizations.
>
> I personally, however, am not inclined to accept the historian's account as final. I would much rather go on believing that some day this common ground will be discovered, since it must necessarily be there. In the meantime, we shall wait with the expectation that the indication by the mystic will lead to that discovery.

The question that was now raised referred to further elucidation of the theory of conflict, and it was raised by the minister of the church, who was now in a more placid mood than before.

> If conflict must imply a whole community, with definite spheres of agreement and disagreement in it, do the Search people really imply that if the sphere of disagreement must produce negative results, it still does not follow that the whole of the community must on that account come to dissolution? Do they want the meeting to realize, then, that the sphere of agreement will still survive? And if, for the sake of argument, one holds that the sphere of agreement has a definite function to work out — say, conceiving or formulating the objective of the community — will that function still continue to be discharged? Finally, if the discharge of that function means a definite, organized life for fulfilling what are known as common interests in a community, do they mean that that organized life need not be affected by the completely negative results in the sphere of conflicting interests?

The people of the Search felt greatly inspired by this question and their reply was very much to the point.

> We are confident that the negative results will not involve the whole community, as the minister and perhaps the secular historian, too, feels that they might. And the reason for this conviction is that an objective cannot be at the mercy of the modes of activity by which it is to be realized. It stands unique and independent. So that failures, if they are inevitable, can only mean that the objective still remains unfulfilled. As a matter of fact history has been a record of failure and not of success: but would anyone argue on that ground that the universe had in any sense come to an end without even the tiny human species within its vast range surviving? Perhaps failures, too, have a meaning in the scheme of the universe. In any case the worst that ever happened to an objective as a result of the failure to realize

> it was confusion in men's minds as to how to bring about its fulfilment.

The Search people were emphatic in their assertion that the three civilizations — based on group, class and community — never disappeared from history, even though none of them ever succeeded in fulfilling their main objectives.

> The conceptions of unity, individuality and community have never as yet been disowned or discarded by any of their votaries. Today they stand exactly as they ever did and no fresh conception has usurped their places. Even the confusion on the level of ultimate conflict did not lead to their extinction. The issue, however, is very complicated and we may have to wait for its solution till we arrive at the Truth to which the Search is moving on.

It was already getting beyond the long twilight hour and soon the lemon blush on the horizon would fall asleep and dream of the great meeting in the mountains. The people who sat listening the whole evening felt as if the whole village was preparing to go with the Search. Some of the elders, at least, did join the Search. That night the lake anxiously watched a change in the moods of the mountains. It was by sheer chance that they did not drop her on the earth by drawing in for a long salute their outstretched arms in which the lake lay fast asleep.

But there was no commotion in the house where the people of the Search slept; the Royalties, the Jesuits and the people of the Search all slept soundly and in perfect peace.

4

As, in the nature of things, the Search came to be known more and more widely and people in the distant cities and towns got all sorts of strange reports about its aim and achievement, it soon found itself directly within the orbit of the Peace Movement that followed the Second World War. One day as it was moving on from place to place in the usual way it was suddenly approached by an excited group of men and women with an appeal that the Search should spend a little time at least with the representatives of the great Peace Movement. These representatives, the Search was told, came from all quarters, not only from the world of science, art and literature but also from that of thought, devotion and action. At least some of them who were well-known international figures had dedicated their lives to this movement. And yet perhaps it was the millions in the movement who would give them an idea of its real stature. And as if all this vivid account might still fail to stimulate the people of the Search to cultivate the Peace Movement, those who approached the Search in an extremely earnest spirit kept on repeating to them that peace had come to the human home at last. The miracle had happened though it was not yet known to the states of the Western world.

There was certainly no reason why the people of the Search should not accept the invitation to discuss the great issue of peace with the leaders of that great movement. The Search itself was out for peace, since Truth was their objective. It was only natural, then, that there should be no dissenting voice in the Search — not even the ministers of the church or the secular historians stood out in opposition to the acceptance of the invitation. Since what is called politics was of no consideration to any of them, it was perfectly easy for the whole Search to fall in with the appeal from the peace people.

It was in a beautiful medieval city somewhere in the hinterland of Asia and not very remote from the border of Europe that a meeting was arranged between the people of the Search and the leaders of the movement for peace. And when in due time the Search people moved on towards the city even the far approach to it made them instantly sensitive to the air that the city unmistakably breathed. It had never been so pure as now and though, at least, to some it was still in part medieval in its pungent feel, there was nothing offensive in it. It was really very bracing indeed.

Like the change in its surrounding air the differences both in its proportion and visible equipment stood out frankly to any observer of the city. If the old folk were still alive in spite of these changes, they were certainly not moving about as they used to do, even half-a-century ago. The style in the movement of the present generation is by no means an echo of the past; every man and woman has a look in his or her eyes which is not altogether heavenward. Not one of them quite fails to take due notice of what is happening on this earth.

Strangely, however, the very ancient habit of expecting things to happen is still very active and perhaps there is no man or woman who is not intently harking back to the past as their forefathers did. Perhaps it is not possible for any people on earth not to look for their true type if it be a fact that they lost it some time in their long, chequered past.

But would the city keep its present ultra-modern shape for long, let alone for ever? Is this the final shape of its real life, which as it were in one bound removed its age-long servitude and created a surging spirit of freedom in its place?

There are many who hold that the city will discard in time the whole of that feature which came recently from the West. But nobody suggests that it will, in consequence, even by mistake lapse back into the old lethargy of spirit which long servitude to the state or to the Church produced. It is another matter whether it will choose a foreign model as a permanent trait — that it will never do.

But the fact is that the future is still unborn, whether in this city or in any other known to us. The issue is not whether this city will settle down to a way of life which is neither indigenous to it nor capable of solving all life's problems. But it will certainly not leave this way so long as it has not drawn from it sufficient vital strength to rise to the normal level of life from which it has long been cast out.

As the Search people came up to the city gates the leaders, who were waiting for them, took them straight to a very famous hall where soon a rich banquet was held.

And when the banquet was over it was arranged that they should meet the next day to find out exactly how the two movements, the Search for Truth and the Movement for Peace stood to one another and what the points in common between them were. Some of them even felt that they might join hands and form one whole movement out of the two.

The case for the Peace Movement was opened by a world-famous scientist and, strangely enough, he made it without once referring to what actually happened to the millions who had suffered in the war. As if all that grim experience had to be taken only as an episode which the historian would some day record: there seemed to be no other alternative. He spoke naturally only of the present and its inevitable bearing upon the future and whatever statements he made derived their force and appeal from simple, indisputable facts. There was nothing which he said for which evidence was not given and the conclusion that he drew on the basis of this evidence was, to his mind, the only conclusion that could be drawn. There could not be a more objective presentation of a case for peace — at any rate that was the view of the scientists present.

What the seientist took special care to point out was that the human species in the twentieth century after a rather long, winding march through history has almost reached a stage of existence in which it may be called upon at any moment to revert even to its pre-human form if it is not careful.

> There is definite prospect today that the whole framework of civilized and semi-civilized existence may be completely destroyed. And the evidence for this is to be found in the simple fact of the presence of atom bombs in the armoury of the two most powerful states in the world today. If the two states go to war the chances are that they would not return from that war to rebuild their civilizations. What type of human species will still survive and how long it will take that species to re-establish civilization is an idle and academic issue. No scientist worth the name is interested in that issue.
>
> If, however, it seems to be extremely undesirable that the twentieth century should have to witness the suicide of the human race, the twentieth-century man has to discard warfare as a means of establishing peace. It is no longer even a question of arguing with the states to prove to them how warfare today is like fire which can only reduce whatever it touches to ashes. They will simply have to drop it unless by a plan of the universe the return of the forest age and the glacial age is falling due again. If, still, the states have to indulge passions or seek redress for wrongs done or destroy what they regard as evil, they will have to choose some other means to achieve their purpose than warfare.

> There can be no excuse for them to preserve warfare any longer — they have to abolish it altogether.

The scientist spoke as if he had just discovered a Law of Nature which does not wait on the decision of mere states as to whether it will have its place in the universe or not, and proceeded:

> The issue, today, no longer rests with states but with what should be called the Law of Nature. It would be stupid to believe that nature is what the scientist makes her out to be. If the scientist had any real control over the birth of nature, he would have long ago manufactured the atom bomb. Jesus Christ would not have had to die on the Cross, as the Christians might well argue. There would have been at least some scientists about at the time to produce the atom bomb, if only to destroy the Pharisees. The fact is that the atom bomb is a twentieth-century natural phenomenon. There is no feature of a revelation in it either from the Mystical Unity or from the Personal God; nor can it be classified under the Platonic Idea or identified with the pagan divinity. It is a phenomenon of nature, as the twentieth-century man chooses to define reality if he happens to be a scientist. Neither ethics nor what has been known as ideal or purpose can by any chance question its claim. The scientist obeys the Laws of Nature and no state has the capacity to legislate against nature. Both of them have to abide by those laws.
>
> The atom bomb is nature's latest form of appearance. It means that human civilization is no longer standing erect but is entirely at the mercy of nature — whether it will survive another day it is for nature, not the states or the gods, to decide. In one second, as it were, the faiths and beliefs which built up our social framework in the course of long centuries have been almost miraculously swept away. Indeed, what is ruling the universe today is not human mind or spirit but their direct opposite, matter or atom bomb. What the scientist has done is only to convey this message to the states. It is for the states to

> decide before it is too late whether they should close down the temples and churches in which the Absolute Spirit or the Divine Man is still worshipped, and revive instead, with fervent appeal for forgiveness, the worship of Nature.

At this stage of the argument the philosopher, on behalf of the Search people, sought for further information and intervened with a question. "Does the great scientist," he asked, "really imply that the human social order, in whatever form, is practically moribund today and is no longer functioning? How could it escape such disruption if all the faiths and beliefs which served it as its basis have failed to meet the challenge from the atom bomb? If the human race is on the eve of reinstating the worship of Nature in some way akin to that of our ancient forbears, could we help concluding that we have absolutely reached the stage of confusion in what we call our civilized existence?"

To this the scientist replied:

> As a scientist I am not in a position to discuss questions which raise implications behind what we call our experience, which is immediate and direct. These implications may, and perhaps do, range over a vast area of what we call our universe but they are not amenable to treatment by the methods we, as scientists, employ. We are concerned with only the most immediate implications which we call by the name of hypotheses. And even there if we actually do leave the direct path of immediate experience and move into shadowy realms, we do so with full conviction that we have a chance of verifying our theories in the end. We do not even hesitate nowadays to utilize rather too often our next-door neighbour, the mathematician, but even in such a case we provide for the safeguard that we shall in the end finish up on the plane of common sense or verification.

> There is, however, no reason why I should not draw the conclusion from the premises I have suggested which the philosopher really wants me to draw. It is certainly not possible that the human social order can exist side by side with the atom bomb which is its direct contradiction. The fact is that the social order does no longer exist — the evidence for this will be found in at least the all-encompassing sense of insecurity throughout the whole world. Even those who are intent on building and not merely destroying, by trying to make believe that the atom builds just as much as it destroys, are not free from this nervousness which a sense of insecurity necessarily breeds. Besides even if they still confidently think that there is such a thing as the justice of history which is sure to preserve the social order of man, the question whether the atom bomb will prevail is not very much affected by the claim of justice. It is very difficult to draw a line on the basis of that concept alone. Indeed if the social order is not exactly under a pall of smoke at the moment, there are signs that it will soon be reduced to a shambles if the universe does not quickly replace the decrepit order of tradition by quite a different type.
>
> I agree with the philosopher that there is nothing to go by if we follow tradition; we have literally reached a stage of universal confusion. The atom bomb would not have arrived in the twentieth century if that century had not staged scepticism all over the human world. We really have no faith or ambition left except that we still refuse to be killed by the enemy. We feel we would much rather commit suicide.

But before the scientist finished his argument there was almost a commotion in the rank and file of the Peace people. It was evident that the opinion of the scientist, whatever its authority, was by no means endorsed by all. No doubt, like the scientist, they all wanted peace and would abolish warfare at any cost;

but they did not agree with him that the main issue was one of transforming the social order of man. On the contrary a considerable number of them frankly held that the issue of peace would be solved automatically provided we ruled out the atom bomb and brought about complete disarmament.

"It is simply not true," they said, "that the atom bomb is a direct evidence of universal confusion. What, indeed, has the Law of Nature got to do with the Law of Mind and Spirit? Surely it is not Nature which rules the universe but Spirit. And if, still, the human species does seem to be facing possible disaster today that is only an evidence that it has deviated from the right path and must be brought back to the life of the spirit."

The reply to this, however, did not come from the scientist but from the philosopher of the Search people.

"If we want peace," the philosopher said:

> as we all do, we have to find out at least two things — the ways and means to remove obstacles from the path of peace, and the ways and means by which we can construct and establish peace. And it so happens that these two conditions are quite distinct. One of them clearly is altogether a negative process. It calls upon us frankly only to remove the obstacles. And it is a familiar truth that the result of such a process, if successful, is disappearance of the obstacles. The other, on the contrary, is a positive process. It calls upon us to posit and affirm the construction of peace. The result, if it succeeds, is the appearance of peace.
>
> Nobody need question the view of the scientist that the atom bomb is at least an obstacle in the path of peace, an obstacle so great that peace may not come back to the social order of man again. And if it is still open to us to doubt the judgement of the scientist we have to note that he is the only authority we have on the Laws of Nature. It may still be that he is by some chance mistaken but certainly we have no help for the

suffering that the mistake will indisputably cost us. And it is a fact that the mistakes of the scientist always correspond to the mistakes which the philosophers, the divines and the statesmen all equally make. There will be no point, therefore, in merely harping on mistakes, whatever their consequences.

But if we have to believe that obstacles in the path of peace have actually arisen with the appearance of the atom bomb, it is neither here nor there to argue about the source from which the atom bomb has come. We may not even be able to decide whether it is Nature or Spirit which is the presiding genius of the universe or whether history has been nothing but a clash between them. We may simply fail to trace the source and origin of the atom bomb. There is the whole record of history to bear this out.

Can we possibly argue that nothing has happened to the social order of man if we have to admit that there is a positive obstacle in its path as a direct result of the manufacture of the atom bomb? And if such a supreme obstacle has actually arisen will it not mean necessarily a hold-up all along the line of our civilized life? Can we possibly deny that? It can only mean to us that the machinery of social order is not functioning as it normally does. And the only issue to discuss after that misfortune is, what could this sudden change in our social order possibly imply? Perhaps we can find out. This is the negative process of removing obstacles.

It seems to be obvious that this change can only mean the state of impasse. And this conclusion follows if we at all know the nature of the way in which the machinery of our social order functions. There are two points which we must note as essential to that knowledge: the social order functions always in a state of conflict, whether external or internal; and to function is to try to establish one or other of the two values between which the conflict lies. It follows, therefore,

> that if and when a social order stops functioning no value is being established at the moment and that is exactly what is meant by the state of impasse, which is another name for confusion.
>
> And if we have to admit that all beliefs and faiths today are necessarily in confusion, surely our faiths in either Spirit or Nature will not survive. It would be meaningless to expect after this that either Spirit or Nature would somehow prevail to remove the obstacle or to suggest at this late hour that it is either the one or the other that still rules the universe.
>
> Yet the strangest part of the whole story is that the atom bomb is not merely an evidence of confusion in the human social order; it has to be taken as an evidence of confusion in the realm of Nature too. That which is capable of destroying everything is almost under an obligation to destroy itself. It is another name for the situation which the absolute sceptic of human history tried to envisage in the shape of "Nothing is".

"But does it really follow that the human social order is not functioning at all even if we cannot deny that we are busy in manufacturing the atom bomb? And what about the 'cold warfare' or its hot defence? Is that a state of confusion too?" some of the Peace people most impatiently asked the philosopher.

The philosopher in reply said:

> Certainly we may be even furiously acting while we are carrying on a cold war or manufacturing atom bombs. There can be no question about our activity at the moment. But the issue is not whether we are still active or altogether dead. The issue is whether our social order is still functioning. If the cold war or our punctilious care to manufacture atom bombs is a sure sign that we are not dead it need not be an evidence that we are active in the sense in which we normally are when the social order is functioning. In other words our activity at the moment is not directed towards

> negating a social value in the interest of its opposite or reconstructing it after its opposite has been completely suppressed. It is taking place, on the contrary, in a strange situation in which it is sought to negate both the values at the same time. And what is more the two sides to the conflict have practically equal chances of destroying one another. We have to note that a social order when it functions normally makes room for the independent existence of either one side or the other, or one value or the other, and for either destruction or construction. But the cold war implies the presence of equally efficient exertion on both sides to destroy one another and of no construction whatsoever.
>
> Should we still claim that our social order is functioning? And if it is not functioning, would it be right to question the conclusion that at least it is in confusion or fairly on the way to it?

There was no reply to this from the dissenting members of the Peace Movement but the scientist here put a question to the philosopher.

> Does the philosopher imply that even the prelude to atomic warfare means also a stage of radical change in the atomic field in which the atoms themselves must clash as opposites and divide themselves into opposite realms with the sure prospect of confusion arising in the atomic field?

The philosopher answered that it did; but to do justice to this answer the whole theory of the physical universe would have to be revised. That revision was beyond the comprehension of all tradition and not exactly relevant to the present meeting. "But the Search people believed," added the philosopher, "that by the time they got to the Truth, as indicated by the Mystic, all these issues would be resolved."

5

There was no further talk on the issue of the competing claims of Nature and Spirit but another section of the Peace people raised another very important issue with reference to the nature of society. The philosopher was asked: "Would it be at all correct to say that history till today has been nothing but conflict between three incompatible social schemes?" which seemed to be his central position. Some of the people in the Peace Movement suggested by way of challenge that if conflict be a fact, it does not appear between three schemes but between two classes: the owning class and the class that has always stood dispossessed. The direct implication of this position is that there is only one human social order and not three, or even two; and this social order has always stood divided into two sections — the section that has owned the wealth and means of production, and the section that has had no wealth nor any control over the means of production. If the latter still has the means of subsistence which at times is reduced to the minimum level or liable to be even altogether absent, it is procured in exchange for the services they render by their labour. It so happened that the "tools of production did not work themselves, nor could they be worked by those who owned them. Why it was so is another question, but it was so."

They further added that the two sections within the same social scheme had been in perpetual conflict during long centuries and the result of the conflict had marked invariably the suppression of the class which did not own the means of production.

> The change from this stark historic situation, however, came at last and it came only when the Communist State appeared as a gift from the greatest revolution in history, in the twentieth century. If the dispossessed class during the last 3,000 years had the status only of slaves, serfs or proletariat, the last revolution almost by a miracle put them in the position of the ruling class. The conflict between them thus came to an end and in the place of two classes of history one class only came to constitute the social scheme in the Communist State. It is now only a question of time before the still surviving 'Class States' will evolve the Communist framework. How then could the philosopher describe history in terms of a clash between three distinct social schemes which perpetually clashed and produced only confusion in the end? There has been conflict in history, no doubt; and this took place in a body social, since the individuals were social beings, but they belonged to the same social scheme and professed the same economic necessity as their paramount need. They did not belong to separate social schemes as if they were different types of individuals and had different paramount needs. Could we possibly conceive of different economic needs? Even the animal world did not choose to differ from the human species on the score of economic needs.

In reply to these Communists the philosopher admitted at once that there had been in history what they described as the conflict between classes, and that it was also true this conflict had appeared without fail inside the body politic of all the three social schemes he had referred to.

> None of the three schemes, as they proceeded to realize their specific objectives, escaped this internal conflict since the objectives, as a matter of course, admitted of two opposite

> ways of realization. The final result, however, did not precipitate the permanent victory of either of them but a state of confusion in which the whole community in question ceased to function for a time.

The philosopher earnestly referred the Communists to the record of the Search for an account of conflict as such. He begged them to remember that even the dialectic which their position implied did not minimize the value of opposition in the shape of contraries. If their leader still chose to repudiate Hegel, he gave no reason for that choice.

> The fact is that conflict takes two forms: one of contradiction, one of contrariety. If conflict is admitted at all, it has to be admitted with its full scope and range. There is no reason to hold that the proletariat will from now prevail till the universe comes to a close any more than that there is evidence that the slave really became a serf and then a proletarian or remained exactly what he was, a slave. Nor is it a fact that the owning class did not undergo a change corresponding to the changes in the position of the working class as slave, serf and proletarian.
>
> What actually happened was that the slave, the serf and the proletarian functioned as members of three separate social schemes — the Classical humanistic scheme, the Medieval community scheme and the Modern individualistic scheme. They did not form continuous history, since the schemes were incompatible with one another.
>
> These three schemes belonged to European history. There was at least one other history, the Asian, which was quite distinct from any of the three forms of European history. How then could we claim that history evolved only one social scheme? Could we repudiate fact if our sole concern were to interpret history? Could we deny that if the slave appeared only in Classical history, the Classical social scheme in which he appeared existed and functioned only in Classical times and not at all in the medieval or modern?

The serf is neither the slave nor the proletarian, exactly as the proletarian is not the slave or the serf. They are altogether different people and belong to different social schemes and appear in different epochs of history. The relation between them cannot be accounted for by any theory of evolution, since the three forms of social schemes cannot be classified under any one type. The Classical and the Medieval are frankly incompatibles; while the Classical and the Modern, though they both belong to the humanistic type, are altogether differently oriented. And if we cannot classify them under any one head it would be useless to account for them by a theory of progressive evolution, even if we grant for the sake of argument that that theory is still somehow in vogue.

What is the point, then, of cutting down the proportions of history, assuming that that is the only way to establish the Communist account of history? Even if we do not enter the realm of speculation we have sufficient data for the conclusion that the history of Europe during at least the last 3,000 years developed two distinct social schemes, of which the one known as humanism appeared in two distinct forms. That accounts for the fact that the internal clash in each of them produced the slave and the slave owner, the serf and the lord of the manor, and the proletarian and the plutocrat. If there is no chance of classifying the schemes it is equally impossible to classify the slave, the serf or the proletarian. Finally, this account of social schemes is relevant only to European peoples and leaves well alone the Asian scheme which is a different social order altogether.

The issue, again, is not merely whether the slave, serf or the proletarian belonged to the same social scheme. One has also to notice that the Classical scheme was superseded by the Medieval, even as the Medieval was replaced by the Modern. So that both the slave and the slave owner were equally superseded by the serf and the lord of the manor. But this replacement did not take place until the internal economy in the Classical scheme had reached a stage of

> impasse, as a result of perpetual conflict between the slave and the slave owner. It is a fact of history that the slave of one age became the slave owner of the next and it was only when adjustments had taken place in the name of justice that the stage of impasse or contrariety was reached. This is known in history as the stage of distintegration or stagnation — a stage which exposes the social scheme in question to invasion from the outside world and its final reduction to slavery.

"But certainly," the Communists still argued, "the Communist State has made steady, rapid progress since its inception, as a result of which the large mass of the proletariat, which was sunk in poverty for ages untold, has for the first time in history got its chances in life." Would the philosopher object to all this as reactionary? Should we, again, discard the opportunities for the production of the necessities of life or for providing for comforts, immunity from diseases and from cataclysms of nature which the sciences alone in the twentieth century have made possible?

> What then is his ground for holding the view that there has been nothing in the life which we have lived so far which could establish peace and avoid confusion?

The philosopher said in reply:

> It will be cynicism to object to the satisfaction of human needs, whether in the shape of amelioration of suffering or provision for the fulfilment of life. If I have joined the Search for Truth my reason for doing so is that it may show us the way by which we can really get out of what may be called the mazes of life: the supreme instance of such a maze appeared when we periodically fell into the illusion that we had at last discovered the way of living in peace. There was, at such moments, absolute faith that poverty was gone for good and joy would mark the horizon of our future for ever and ever. What we call the positive achievement of civilizations or what still are regarded as records of the

brilliant past are the extant evidences of such moments.

But can anybody deny that the bright and brilliant past not only did not illuminate our life for long but was bought at the expense of at least another brilliance which belonged to our opponents? When we switched on the light in our newly-decorated hall as the guests arrived, our opponents had to switch off the light from their decorated hall and leave their guests in utter darkness. And what did really happen in the end? How did we stand to one another? We all lost faith — even in our gods — sooner or later and entered into darkness; and it was so dark all around that we knocked our heads against the surrounding walls and actually fell into a swoon.

The question is not, then, whether the Communist State is producing food enough to feed the starving millions or increasing the chances of joy for them. They are doing wonders. And in all their achievement certainly it is modern science which is helping them and its method is one of conscientiously extracting the goodness of life on which our earth, air and water have for untold ages survived. And as the age of plenty and abounding life matures, treasures will be collected in abundance in the shape of new arts and crafts to delight the heart of these millions.

All this, however, whatever its value, by no means reads like a fairy story. Even if mountains are moved from their bases and the long arms of the seas are bent or prolonged to recover fertile lands from their hidden beds or bring the world of submarine life to minister more sumptuously than ever to the needs of the human race, and even if the earth grows more food and larger varieties of it than ever before to satisfy the hungry men and the well-stocked animals for man's need and enjoyment, it will not be achieving anything of a kind which never was achieved before. The mountains have been moved periodically by the earthquakes according to a cosmic schedule which laid out the beds afresh on which the seas and rivers were to flow, and if nature wanted a bumper crop there was a bumper crop, whatever happened.

> These are not exceptional events whatever the way in which they may have been brought about.
>
> But is this the way in the name of history to solve the question of peace, which must provide food for the whole human race and for the animal world too, and not merely for the autocrat or the democrat, the capitalist or the Communist, the Brahmin or the Buddhist, the Platonist or the Atomist, the Catholic or the Protestant? How long, again, will science reign as it has been reigning for, say, a couple of centuries? Some say that it is already on the wane. Have we got any assurance yet from our scientists that they do at last know the true nature of the physical universe and will not have to change their conception of it again? These are cardinal issues for those who are growing food today or moving mountains. The issue is not one of producing food for some and for a time: but for all and for all time.
>
> The truth which still shines in these periodic outbursts of glory, however, is that they do minister to the cause of justice, if not of peace. The vast millions who have been starving have a right to be fed; and it makes no difference if science, by quite a mistaken theory of the physical universe, feeds them. Even if the whole of all this achievement and glory is found sooner or later to be but a castle in the air based on pure illusion, it still has to be conceded a value. It serves the purpose of justice — perhaps the only value that history has known so far.

"But I want peace," the philosopher said, "and not justice. It is possible for me to pass by justice on the way and move on for peace. I want the Communist not to forget history."

Some of the Search people at this stage took great pains to point out that the Peace Movement was not even based on an original idea of peace which they all so devoutly wanted.

Evidently they had not raised the issue whether the human mind ever really knew what it wanted when its main objective was peace. It seemed to be obvious that the Peace people meant by peace simply what the Hindus or the Christians or the Humanists had meant by it. It did not strike them that there were necessarily three distinct types of peace which were implied by the three distinct organizations. Moreover, as these organizations clashed with one another the three notions of peace necessarily also clashed.

Perhaps a more correct way of assessing the significance of this movement would be to emphasize the stand for the abolition of the atom bomb and disarmament. But that would imply only a negative conception which might be of no avail unless there were a fresh, positive notion of peace. Perhaps, somehow, the Peace people believed that once war were abolished it would be possible for Hindus, Christians and Europeans to live together in peace. But the most gruesome fact of history was that if there had been warfare it was due to the very fact that the three types of society, with their claims to absolute Truth, necessarily clashed and produced warfare. If what the Peace Movement wanted wholeheartedly was the abolition of warfare, did it not strike them that warfare could not in the nature of things be abolished if the causes which produced it still survived? Not for a moment did they realize that the very conception of peace in tradition was the fundamental cause of warfare: and it was necessary that they must abandon this before anything could be achieved in the way of abolishing warfare. The sooner this was realized the better would it be for the Peace Movement.

Without a doubt it was the scientist who struck the correct note when he said that warfare as a technique of living was no longer available to man if he did not wish to revert to primitive conditions.

> The presence of the atom bomb cannot but imply the absence of all values on which the social order of man has so far rested. If, today, the scientist has been the medium through whom Nature registered a challenge to the whole framework of life and necessarily to all the values that it cherished, the Hindu, the Christian and the European will lose their claim even to common sense if they still hark back to their respective traditional ways of guaranteeing peace in the human family.

Still, as the philosopher pointed out, if there was anything remarkable in tradition, it appeared in what he had already described as justice. No civilization ever had its own way all the time and none escaped the tribulation of defeat. And this judicious balance was preserved even with regard to peace and warfare. If history has been a venue for warfare, it has been a venue also for peace. If all metaphysic defined Reality in terms of both Being and non-Being, the organization which was built on it provided also for both the Negative and the Positive. It made room for peace which served for the Positive or Being as well as for warfare which served for the Negative or non-Being. It would be unfair and wrong to make an apotheosis of peace and rule out warfare as the only blot on the universe.

> If we want to abolish warfare, we have to abolish peace as well; or if we want to establish peace, we have equally to establish warfare. A strange thing to say, no doubt, but there is no alternative if we want to face truth. We have to discover a way of life in which there will be provision for both peace and warfare although of quite a different kind.

The philosopher insisted that perhaps the Truth which the Mystic indicated might give us the real clue at last.

The Peace Movement was very greatly impressed indeed and most of the erudite and earnest members of it decided to join the Search. The result was that the Search by now became a very formidable body. In fact, the only sections of the community who still were not represented in it were the orthodox religious bodies, the states and the seats of learning. Even if they were in confusion, they chose to carry on as they had always done, simply to keep things going. The states on whom fell the duty of preserving Western civilization when the long career of its imperial sway was on the wane, seemed to be even hostile to the people who stood for peace and to the Search. They were only partially aware of the split between the East and West and hated the dialectic of history; but they trusted the inorganic world to eliminate the dialectic completely. And it was noteworthy that those states which had raised their fortune partly on the Roman model developed a racialism which even the recent Nordic attempt could hardly beat. The non-white people, in consequence, ceased to exist for them except as buyers of goods in their market or as possible propagandists for their cult — "a strange mixture of iron and soil".

6

The Search now was on the point of resuming the march. But was it the same Search?

It was not the same Search except in one vital feature which was clearly the most central and indisputable. It unmistakably stood united as it always had with reference to its main objective — the search for the Truth as indicated by the Mystic. Those who had joined the Search since its inception held that objective quite as firmly as the original people of the Search did. But the cohesion among the different people in the Search after it had grown enormously in proportion was not of the same strength as it was in its original formation. Perhaps even the faith in the goal of the Search did not take quite the same form in every man or woman who now constituted it. Their common agreement no doubt lay in professing this goal in preference to any other — and nobody questioned the possibility of a realization of this goal — but it was perhaps only the original people who were absolutely certain about its realization.

And so, as a matter of course, the issue soon arose with reference to the constitution of the Search. Evidently a fresh method of dealing with the differences in opinions and habitual reactions in the daily intercourse of life had to be devised. These differences steadily increased as the numbers multiplied and the increase was specially due to the fact that the new people came from diverse and varied cultures and stocks. It was not possible any longer to leave the disposal of these daily increasing problems to the good sense of the people concerned or to the initial inspiration which stimulated the Search. The Search had travelled far from the days of its inception when nothing counted but the Search. The possibilities now were either that the Search, as happens invariably with all fresh movements, sooner or later, would drift back to traditional ways; or that it would have to re-orientate the method of dealing with all such differences. Evidently a constitution was necessary — one which had to be quite original and fresh. It was inconceivable that the Search would maintain its integrity and at the same time follow either the autocratic or democratic method, which as a matter of course destitutes or suppresses one of the interests in dispute for the sake of the other. An altogether new technique of dealing with differences had to be found the Search in its purity was expected to continue its course.

And at such a crucial stage the committee which in due course was appointed formulated a whole system of ethics bearing on the issue of differences. This ethics suggested a completely new procedure in reference to the way of dealing with conflicting interests, no matter what the sphere in which they appeared or on what scale. In it the techniques which tradition followed — force or persuasion, and when those failed, compromise — were completely superseded by a new technique.

Yet the principle on which this new ethics was based was already a familiar principle to the Search. The people of the Search had discovered this principle as a result of the long deliberations which took place in the mountain retreat. It was the fresh analysis of the nature of conflict and the discovery from it that both sides in a conflict were equally in illusion which gave them the clue to that principle. They had seen that the interests in a conflict, inasmuch as they were equally illusory, did not admit of realization but implied instead mutual abstention.

Accordingly the new ethics was called the "ethics of mutual abstention" and without any controversy was unanimously accepted by the whole body of the Search. Even the divines and the secular historians abstained from raising any difficulty as to its acceptance. And the grounds on which they accepted it were partly because the new ethics was an altogether fresh mode of dealing with conflicts and partly, perhaps, because all traditional ethics stood for nearly the same thing though according to the divines they failed to give expression to their views. The basis of the constitution for the Search was thus well laid.

The Search by now stood in complete detachment from all existing societies since it had developed a constitution which excluded both warfare and persuasion as methods of solving conflicts. It could not, even by mistake, be described as a body which professed either autocracy or democracy — it recognized instead both the values of unity and individuality. It was indeed the first society known in history which stood for absolute equality whether in conflict or harmony. And as a direct consequence of this it took both the values or interests in a conflict as equally illusory. Neither unity nor individuality as we have so far understood them survived as a value. In fact, the conception of standard dropped out altogether. Neither spirit nor matter, for instance, between which the clash always lay in all tradition was regarded as absolute. And so it followed that all the three organizations, Hindu, Greek and Christian, since they were found to be in a state of perpetual clash had to be taken as cherishing illusory objectives.

If still no fresh organization had yet been proposed by the Search to take their place, two features stood out as ultimate and fundamental in the main scheme of its constitution: the common purpose, which was the beacon that had been lighted by the Mystic, and the way of dealing with conflicts by mutual abstention rather than by violence, by non-violence or by compromise.

Evidently these features of its constitution were bound to make the Search a stupendous movement; and as such it might at any moment assume the proportions of a challenge to the states, to the seats of learning and to the centres of orthodox faith. Even if there was nothing on the face of it which might be taken as in any way offensive to the states the fact was that it was steadily depleting the strength of the states, by drawing upon the manpower and moral support on which they survived. It was not possible that the Search and the states could collaborate with such completely different techniques as warfare and mutual abstention or live together within the same social economy in perfect peace.

But what exactly happened at this stage in the relationship between the Search and the state is a matter for surmise, since there is no historical record available.

There is no evidence that the Search was even temporarily broken up by the state, or that the states, leaving aside all their domestic and international troubles, actually waged a kind of war against the Search; no such step could be taken precisely because there was no common universal reaction to the Search from all the existing states. It was evident that the states in Asia which stood for justice, dignity and peace felt that the Search could by no means be out of tune with them inasmuch as it frankly recognized the place of justice in history. If Truth and peace in the human family were its avowed goal, the Eastern states held that such a peace could not arrive till justice had been done and dignity restored. The West had to recognize the East as its equal by shedding its historic pride and gracefully abandoning the "possessions" which did not belong to it by any right.

It was another story how this equalization in status could be brought about. It was certainly not the business of the Search people to take any part in such matters: they were by their whole outlook detached from all existing social orders, since their interest was to provide for the future of the whole human race, rather than for some section of it at the expense of some other. But what would happen to the Search if war should arise between the Western and the Eastern states? The answer was that it could not arise; it was precluded by the very nature of the existing split between them. Besides, if one goes by the trend of history, it is not iron and steel but justice which is foreshadowed as the only legitimate factor for determining the scope of the immediate future. If, indeed, the Western states could still believe that they had a right to win in any warfare against the Eastern states they would have to match the claim for justice by a much superior claim before they would be able to realize that right. The iron-and-steel which appears to be their only stock-in-trade cannot possibly supply that claim: it is questionable whether it can even help the Western states for any length of time to keep order among their own peoples. War between the Eastern and Western states therefore seems to be out of the question.

A meeting was, however, immediately convened to consider whether in any circumstances the Search could run the risk of being entangled with the state. It so happened, however, that it was almost immediately interrupted by the arrival of some leading personalities from the Western states anxious to revive the Conference, which had for some time been in abeyance. Their arrival was greeted cordially since the object of these notabilities was to find out if the Search could bring about a settlement between the East and the West. They were genuinely anxious for peace and did not in any sense advocate the policy of the states which was based on the technique of warfare. They were convinced that warfare was incapable of bringing about any appreciable change for the better: it could only repeat the lessons of the long past.

But strangely enough they had not only kept away rigidly from the Peace Movement but had chosen to carry on as law-abiding members of their state; and the explanation of this seeming paradox was that they had a strong sense of personal dignity which served them as the ethics for their life. What was clear to them was that they could not stand in the way of either the state or the Peace Movement: they were in duty bound to follow the state and the Peace Movement as, periodically, the one or the other prevailed. They had no choice, since they had no standard or principle to put in the place of that which either the state or the Peace Movement professed. They accepted the state and the Peace Movement because they were the only creations of history which sponsored human interests. They had to be served as a matter of conscience, whatever the suffering and misery such a service might mean to all concerned. Even if the life of order or that of peace in its true form had not so far been achieved in the human home, it was not for them to withhold their services, since they had nothing to put in the place of peace and order. This is what they understood by the notion of personal dignity, the last stronghold of the human individual. In their opinion not even suffering could break through this stronghold.

Yet theirs was not a case of martyrdom. There was no spiritual flavour in it. It was the high watermark of individualism, if anything, based upon the conception of immortality; which was another name for individuality to them.

7

In good time a special Meeting between these highly sophisticated personalities and the people of the Search took place, and that quite informally in a gracefully spacious city right in the heart of the continent of Europe. There have been many legends about this city in the archives of Europe which refer to its unearthly features of proportion and grace. No theory, as far as tradition goes, however, has so far quite got the clue as to how one day this city in a strange, sudden mood of disgust and penitence breathed out the whole of its national flavour into the flowing bed of the Seine, which in its turn duly emptied it out into the sea. Nor have perpetual disputes among its historians led to any decision whether its guardian deity, the graceful, gliding Seine, once playfully marked the layout for this city or whether the layout was the result of a sudden, crafty device on the part of an architect to capture her gracious flow. Even now it seems at times that this immemorial flow may rise in a fit of absent-minded gaiety and flood the whole of the layout — and then it will take all the efforts of the million bells in the neighbourhood to quieten her down to her normal bed. What a layout and what a gracious flow!

The Meeting began and as a preliminary the newcomers most anxiously wanted to know what new method the Search people proposed to use in the place of warfare and peace. They had been assured by many that there was a definite method, which could legitimately replace war and peace, in the constitution of the Search. What could be more comforting to the human race than such a prospect today?

It was the philosopher, as usual, who gave the reply at the request of the Search; and he was anxious to share with these learned and earnest folk all that the Search had so far gathered as they kept on meeting people after people of all grades and levels of mature experience.

He mentioned three distinct points, all relevant to the questions that had been raised.

> The people in the Search have sufficient evidence to hold that every man and woman today can conscientiously believe that he or she is an individual being and not a mere creature. There is absolutely no reason why they should not think that they have the capacity to receive messages from the Voices and test them if necessary. And it makes no difference if they have so long been forced to believe that they are mere creatures. The evidence which will help them to shed that illusion has arrived — that is a question of fact. It is another issue why it did not arrive before. That is for the Truth to explain. But once the evidence has arrived it cannot be lost.
>
> The people of the Search, again, on the basis of a fresh review of history have derived a new ethics which makes warfare (whether by violence or by persuasion) useless and unnecessary. That ethics is the ethics of mutual abstention.
>
> Finally, they all have a common faith based on the Mystic's yogic insight, which does not question what we call evidence: and as a result of this common faith the Search is now a full-fledged society with sufficient common interests to hold it together. These interests again do not in the nature of things clash with the interests of any other body.
>
> There are issues, however, which still remain to be solved; one has to find out why history has hitherto appeared to be nothing but a conflict between three organizations without a common background. One cannot accept such a reading

> of history as final, since conflict is impossible without a background of agreement between the conflicting sides. What then can be that background? And, again, if a background is necessary to conflict what can be its relation to fiction, illusion or evil, which have been the main causes of conflict? It is not possible that the human mind can be satisfied with only a universe of conflict, even if one discovers in conflict a new meaning or value. There must be provision in the universe for harmony as well. The answer to these issues we expect will come from the Truth, as the Mystic indicated.

Here was a résumé of what the Search stood for and it proved to be sufficient as a reply to the main question that had been asked. No difficulty was raised and it was possible to proceed to discuss the practical issues: but as a preliminary to this discussion the philosopher took up again the issue of personal dignity. He pointed out that the notion of dignity had three different meanings — which were not only different but necessarily clashed with one other. "Could such highly sophisticated persons," he asked, "mean by dignity something which was not covered by the three notions that are familiar in history? Is it possible that they did not mean by dignity what the mystic or the humanist or the dualist respectively meant by it? And what exactly did they mean when they said that they followed equally the Peace people or the War-lords who alternately prevailed? Could one depend upon one's personal dignity as if it was something like the Absolute and Changeless of tradition? The fact is that there are three historical views and three personal dignities associated with them: and that open and well-marked diversity makes it impossible for any individual to make sure about dignity, since he will be called upon to choose between three brands of it.

The position would be intelligible if one could be absolutely sure of any one of them: but are we sure of any value or view? Do we know, for instance, what are unity, individuality and community, which serve us as our ideal or objectives? Have not perpetual clashes between them reduced them all almost to the status of myths? And what forms have our activities taken if the fact is that we run after fiction or illusion or evil? Have we not been entirely chasing phantasies all our life? How then could dignity alone of all the values survive? It would do us at least some good to know that the total result, in the end, of all history has been scepticism, which also in its turn has had to suffer a demise. Could the claim of the sophisticated possibly rest on the score of what they call personal dignity? To what school of thought, in the last analysis, do they owe allegiance, or do they propose to initiate a school of their own?"

There was an attempt on the part of some of those present to define dignity in terms of democratic freedom and personality. But this did not cut much ice with the rest, since such freedom was evidently at the cost of unity and order. The discussion here ended and left a definite impression on the newcomers that they had not analysed history sufficiently but had come to a decision on the basis of experience within too limited a horizon. The other point which impressed them about the views of the Search was that here at last was a method of dealing with conflicts which was neither violence nor persuasion but something quite different.

The conclusion they drew from these impressions was that the Search could be accepted provided it did not in any sense clash with the states or seats of learning. This one condition they had still to lay down and it was by no means frivolous or meaningless. If the ground of dignity, as they put it, was not quite tenable, it did not follow that the need for the preservation of the social order was not unimpeachable and necessary. The fact is that suicide in any shape or form was rejected by all the species; even the flamboyant experiment of the sceptic to involve the whole of the universe in extinction lacked sufficient space in that universe for its comfortable execution.

And the question that was seriously raised now was whether the ethics of the Search people automatically ruled out any clash between them and the state. And at least one implication of such a question was that the state and the seats of learning, whatever their deficiency, could not be replaced by a vacuum. The Search people must therefore either replace the state by a more efficient body or be scrupulous enough not to interfere with the state.

If the first alternative was ruled out, since the Search constituted a movement for the discovery of Truth and was not in a position to undertake the duties of a government, could they give any guarantee that they would not be in any way interfering with the state? Could they, in other words, claim any privilege from the state which would grant them immunity from mobilization for industry or warfare if necessary?

Normally no group or society of men and women can expect any immunity from mobilization for industry or warfare, since no society can escape the paramount jurisdiction of the state. What special grounds for immunity, then, could be suggested on their behalf by the Search? It seemed that there were only two alternatives: either the Search should convince the state that in its own interest it should leave the Search well alone so that they might cultivate their own way; or they should seek asylum with the animals, who have chosen to preserve their freedom by drawing a line between the forest region and the home of man.

Even there they would not be quite free if by any chance they fraternized with the small groups of their own species on the outskirts of the realm of the animals or sought the high altitudes where the hermits from immemorial times have lived.

The hermits never disowned the state although the latter lived by warfare and persuasion, but the small groups which stood aloof from the hermitage have always lived on the land, which is owned neither by the animals nor by them — a very precarious life indeed! Which of the two courses should they follow if it was inconceivable that they would defy the state? — and their ethics excluded any such defiance. They could not organize a new state, since there were many problems still which they must solve before they could possibly discontinue the Search.

The reply was given by the philosopher, again, and he pointed out that the state ought to grant concessions to the Search, since the latter formed a body of specialists whose main object was to guarantee peaceful construction in human society. "Besides," he said, "if the state does find itself in a mess today and does not know how to solve the split between the East and the West, surely it must be in need of help. In fact, only the other day all the states resorted to the Conference to get their riddles solved. Would it, then, be too much to expect that they would let the Search continue as a body of specialists whose sole object is to solve their riddles for them? And the fact is that the Search has already solved the immediate problem which the Committee of the Conference raised, and has given a review of history to account for the present enigmatic situation in the world."

The sophisticated group persisted, however:

> Will the Search actually succeed in convincing the state about their bona fides? May not the Search fail? Or may not the state miss their point of view and even misunderstand them?

There was no answer to these questions from the philosopher, who refused to dogmatize about future events. He said:

> Perhaps God, if He were here, could answer such questions.

> For the rest of us, who have so far got only the experience of history to go by, all inferences about the future are rigidly conditioned. There have been three forecasts about the future on the basis of three logics; and they have all contradicted one another. No doubt the Search has evolved consistent notions of both, individuality and organization, the two principal factors of social existence. Even the true notion of the ethical principle has been developed by the Search. But these are by no means sufficient to guarantee the validity of what inference we may still have to make about the future. It is not possible, for instance, even to forecast with certainty what the Search people themselves would do if the state suddenly chose to mobilize them for industry and warfare. No doubt we all in the Search have accepted the ethics of abstention and fully believe that we are individual beings and not mere creatures; it is quite another issue how long, under pressure from the state, this conviction would last. The most one could say is that the original people of the Search in all probability would stand the test. And even if they too wavered in the midst of the clash, they would certainly come back to the ethics sooner or later. There can be no certainty about forecasting the future.

"But the main issue," the philosopher continued,

> is not whether the Search is in a position to convince the state that they should not be mobilized for industry and warfare. Perhaps the main issue is whether the state would in any case have to put pressure upon them, in pursuance of their immemorial claim to paramount authority over the whole of the human species: and here one may at least argue that the state need do nothing of the kind. Why, indeed, should we suppose that the state and the seats of learning are bound to act irrationally, as if they are by constitution and temperament the only irrational bodies on this earth? The universe made no discrimination at their birth between races and nations or groups and individuals with reference to their aims and objectives. If there have been three

organizations with three different types they have all had the rational and irrational moments in their career evenly distributed.

If, still, the state should mobilize the Search for industry and warfare there would at least be some grounds for that procedure. And they might well be justified by those grounds — and, what is more, the people of the Search in turn would be tied up with those grounds just as much as the state. The point is that such a compulsion, if it should happen, would surely be an evidence that the Search people were not living up to their ethics and had somehow reverted to traditional types of behaviour. Nobody need be so foolish as to claim that the organization of the Search as it stands is perfect. On the contrary the faiths and beliefs which hold together the people in it are of varied strength by virtue of the fact that they are still attached to the traditions from which they have come, though in varied grades of strength.

If, however, we cannot be certain about the impossibility of a clash between the state and the Search, at least one thing seems to be certain; and that is that the clash will not break the Search for good. On the contrary the total result of this clash will be wholesale conversion of the state to the principle of the Search, sooner or later. After all, the Search has discovered some certainties on which they stand; while the state is wholly absorbed in illusions of the past. The certainties no doubt do not constitute the whole truth but they are not of the type that appear to a mind steeped in illusion which are sure to be contradicted sooner or later. They are absolute.

Then, again, the states do not stand today where they did a century or even half a century ago. Their strength has steadily deteriorated since their opulent days. The two wars and the two dreams left them simply filled with dread. And the total result of the Conference was a split which left at least the Westem states in a state of bewilderment without any policy or principle. Finally, they have lost both manpower and

> moral support by the desertion by vast millions of their programme of warfare; and now even their most sophisticated citizens openly tell us that they have no faith in warfare. Does it not all mean that the state is simply not in a position to come down upon the people of the Search, when it has practically lost its claim to sovereignty by a miserable failure to provide even for the safety of the people. Nobody questions the sovereign authority of the state, whatever its origin. The credit and prestige of the state are not judged today by its origin, these are judged by its capacity to prove them by providing for defence of the body politic and the opportunity for the growth of freedom and joy. Where is that capacity now? Is not the credit maintained by force?

It was as if the Voice was speaking again, though on the other side.

> The issue whether there may be a clash between the state and the people of the Search therefore is not a serious issue. Even if it takes place, it will be organized only by that section of the states which for deep-seated reasons, it seems, has no use for any sustained thought and so has no real policy but only, most surprisingly, an ambition to lead the world. And these exceptional people in the twentieth century may forget, as a matter of sheer fate, that it is not machines or money that will rule any people for long but only a principle or policy, which must be more just and effective than any that went before. And as regards the divine art of making other races in their own image by leadership, it is simply beyond them to exploit it. They have no faith in divinity and they do not know yet what their own image is.
>
> The clash between the people of the Search and the state will not therefore in any case reach any serious level, even if it suddenly and unaccountably breaks out.

8

It was a foregone conclusion that after this review by the philosopher the whole question of reviving the Conference would be dropped. And so instead of pressing for a revival, the newcomers became members of the Search.

The general feeling now was that the Search would go straight ahead to the place where, according to the indication by the Mystic, the Truth was to be found. There was some rejoicing . . . as if the Search had already received the message. Some even felt that the sap of the earth was rising to give them a welcome, and the countryside was coming out to seek their blessings as they did in the past when there was a pilgrimage.

But there was no positive sign yet that the state would join them in a body or that the church bells would ring to announce the advent of the new message or the seats of learning would call their councils to receive the new account of Reality. There was still, somehow, a definite bar between the state and the Search. Either the state ignored the Search or was perhaps waiting for a suitable opportunity somehow to baulk it. The bulk of the community could not come to any decision as to what they should do and continued to "stay put", as if by inertia, where they were. The daily duties were done as usual and what chances life gave in consequence were taken. In fact, there were three distinct trends of life moving in the Western world at one and the same time.

The state and the institutions of learning, culture and faith went on functioning in their usual traditional way.

The bulk of the community moved more or less under their direction in a rather listless way.

The Search marched on towards the unknown horizon as indicated by the Mystic.

It did not, however, follow that these three trends had no common meeting ground. On the contrary the Search, as a constantly moving body with a specific claim, was fully known to the state, exactly as the people were more or less aware of its aims: only even if they knew about one another there was no prospect of any collaboration between the Search and the state. And the people were much too dazed by the pressure of the times to take the initiative to bring the state and the Search together. There was no sign of anything like revolution on the horizon.

The signs that seemed to fill the horizon instead pointed to the dread which seized the state amid all this uncertainty and to the bewilderment of the seats of learning which the two dreams precipitated. The spectre of the Dark Age did not recede and the Far East seemed to be steadily getting more and more menacing. In addition the split was still there to prevent a revival of the Conference.

How long, then, could the state forbear and let the Search go on at the expense of its lifeblood — the manpower and the moral support of the people? Would not time precipitate the need for action, either in the shape of a ban on the Search by constitutional means or some more drastic steps which would suppress the Search altogether? Nobody knew what was going to happen. But something had to happen and it did happen.

A body of strong, virile men, who would easily pass, anywhere, as the core of the diehards, in sheer desperation one day went out and solidly took their stand right on the road on which the Search was moving. They brought a force of armed followers who not only set up barricades but surrounded the Search menacingly. The leaders then threatened that unless the Search returned home or recanted their faith their members would be subjected if necessary to complete annihilation. This was a direct and most unexpected challenge to the Search, which came upon them like a bolt from the blue. In an instant the whole atmosphere had changed. No longer was it one of comparing notes or drawing conclusions on evidence or rejecting hypotheses for want of evidence. Instead it became at once a question of making quick decisions to act in order to live their ideal whatever the consequences.

The immediate effect was a loss of composure, some bewilderment and various movements. But not a single soul of the whole body of the Search hesitated for a moment to apply their new ethical method. There was no attempt to fight back on the part of any: the immediate issue which occupied them in the face of this sudden challenge was to find out what the charge against the Search was or could be. Even the rank and file wanted to know, as they stood unmoved, in what way they had given offence to the state. There was not one who was not prepared to make amends; and in their stand against the challenge there was no sign either of violence or non-violent resistance, only a firm determination to make amends for any wrongs done. The Search took it for granted that they must have given offence by drifting towards some traditional mode of living, as a matter of sheer habit. They could not otherwise account for this sudden challenge to them. It was inconceivable that the way of life they had chosen in the interest of the future of the human race could possibly clash with that of the state or of any institution of the human community.

Nothing came as a reply to their appeal. The real grounds of the siege remained unknown, only a repetition of the threat was made. The Search were told that they were creating disaffection and depleting the manpower and the moral support on which the state subsisted. But this charge did not give any clue as to how they had created the disaffection: if only the facts were known the people in the Search felt convinced that they could completely meet the demand that the besiegers, on behalf of the state, made, without detriment to their ultimate faith.

It was inconceivable that they should disband the whole movement and go back to traditional life. To disband the Search was to commit suicide. It was an impossible act.

The position was indeed extremely difficult and it seemed as if no decision could be taken. Evidently the strain on the Search was growing, as a result of which the rank and file began to waver. Even some of the noted men and women of the Search, especially those who had argued against the Search on religious and secular grounds, were showing signs of impatience with the leaders of the Search. But the core of the Search stood the strain unmoved and undaunted. Nothing overwhelmed the scientist, the philosopher and the original people of the Search: they bore the brunt like a rock, immovable and firm. It was impossible to them that they should either disband the Search or accept the charge of treason against the state made by the representatives of the ruling class. They were simply not in a position to go back on their faith.

Soon, however, a decision was taken as they suddenly realized that they could, at least, go on enduring, unflinchingly and without complaint, the suffering and anxiety and the extreme ignominy which was all the time being heaped upon their heads. That, at least, would be one way of paying for the mistakes they must have made whether they had any sense of them or not.

And they did make this payment to the full; indeed they were prepared for any sacrifice short of disbanding the Search.

But when their payment reached nearly its peak something unexpected happened; the diehards lost their courage. They could not possibly face the necessity of destroying the whole body of the Search and yet they had no alternative since they had not the faintest chance of bending them to their knees. They had the sudden dread that perhaps neither the state nor the people would forgive them for the final act of complete destruction if it were actually to happen. They might have to go into exile for that final act, even assuming that the state granted them pardon. This dread completely overpowered them and they left the whole environment almost in a panic as suddenly as they had come.

Soon there was no trace of them left. . . . As if the Search had endured the nightmare of a siege rather than a real one. It was such a relief and it seemed to them all that there was so much more of freshness in the air and as far as one could see the path ahead of them was straight and spotlessly clear. The Search was on the road again.

What happened to the diehards in the long run is not known; nor is it on record whether those who were impatient and who were for giving in to the diehards still belonged to the Search. These are issues for the historians and no historian has yet answered them.

The Search became, however, much more formidable than ever, especially as it came now to enlist the sympathy and active co-operation of the community on which the state lived and functioned. The people changed, as if they no longer belonged to the state. It was the most momentous occurrence that ever happened in the life of a human community.

There is nothing in the records, however, to show that the Search behaved as did the martyrs or the non-violence resisters when they had to cope with opponents who used force to make them recant their faiths. The Search took ignominy and suffering as their due for wrongs which they must unwittingly have done to their opponents. They saw that the diehards had had to use force: there had been no alternative for them, since they believed in warfare as a legitimate method of removing conflicts and establishing Right in order to provide for Peace. And if the Search did not follow the method of warfare in spite of the fact that its members too were involved in the same conflict with them, the reason was that the Search believed — unlike the diehards — that conflict lay between competing illusions or falsehoods and not between truth and illusion.

It would be utterly pointless in its opinion to fight for illusions — even the diehards would not fight if somehow they could be assured that conflict did not lie between truth and illusion but between contrary illusions. It is extraordinary how the whole of history has missed this simple point.

It is another issue why the people of the Search ran into conflict with the diehards at all. It is one thing to know for certain that conflict can lie only between illusions, a different thing to keep away from conflicts by virtue of this knowledge. The issue of falling into conflict is quite a different thing from that of knowing the nature of conflict. The Search was certainly in a position to act up to its view of conflict if it found itself right in the midst of it but it could not avoid or escape conflict altogether as a matter of choice. After all, the people in the Search were descended from the same stock as their opponents. There would have been no question of their running into conflict with them if they had had an altogether different origin. The two issues — falling into conflict as a matter of inherited interests or desires, and dealing with the conflict after it has arisen — are quite distinct and separate. When, therefore, the Search discovered that the die-hards brought a charge against its members it was clear at once that they must have deviated from the path of the Search and followed wholly illusory ends: from that moment it was bound to be an issue for the Search of making amends for any wrongs done to its opponents and not one of fighting them to preserve those illusory ends. The method of the Search, therefore, if it was frankly the direct opposite of what the diehards followed, was equally remote from the methods of martyrdom and non-violence.

9

Since the total result of the challenge from the diehards definitely led to the renovation of the Search, this naturally put the state in a very awkward position indeed. The renovated Search would be necessarily depleting their manpower and moral support more than ever before, whether the Search wanted it or not. What then would happen to the state? Would the state submit to this process of natural death by attrition or devise some fresh means to preserve their authority at any cost?

It was too early yet for any radical change in the prospects of either the state or the Search. The course of destiny runs by devious ways. The Search, also, did not seek power and authority but left the whole community within the framework of the state exactly as they had found it. And this they could easily achieve since the issue of sovereign authority does not arise with a body like the Search, especially as it laid no claim to be a super-state or even a sphere of activity in which only the spiritual power prevails. The Search was just a normal body of specialists, who wanted to carry on in the interest of the whole of the human community without running into conflict with any section of it; nothing more nor less.

It did not, however, follow that nothing would happen to disturb the equanimity of the state; at least the state would be called upon to answer questions by the people whom they ruled with reference to the two immemorial obligations of the state: defence of the people — which means in the last analysis abolition of warfare — and establishment of peace, which is the only way by which the positive interest of the people can be served.

And as it is certain that the states will fail to satisfy the people on these points they will have to account for their reluctance to accept the method of the Search, which has repudiated warfare and put in its place quite another method. If the method of warfare did not bring peace and security, on what ground could the state still adhere to it? It would no longer be possible for them to make the plea of no alternative.

Nor could the state in the twentieth century deny the right of the people to ask questions. It could not possibly stand any longer on the well-worn claim that it is sacrosanct, as if its authority were divine or even semi divine. It was evident that all such claims were meaningless in the twentieth century: they were of the same kind as the claims made by the spirits which people heard in dreams or saw in visions. If no institution in the twentieth century can expect to survive without the support of the community that support will not be forthcoming unless there is evidence which the human individual is in a position to test. Even the remnants of institutions which claimed divine inspiration, whether mystical or non-mystical, which survive today survive on sufferance from the community. They are not in a position to question the sovereignty of the people and may conceivably be at any moment dismantled if the people so desire it. It is inconceivable that a community of twentieth-century Europe can abide by a dual authority, since division of authority runs counter to its personality, which is indivisible and absolute.

What happened, then, as a matter of fact? What could happen when there was a complete anomaly in the whole situation? The sovereignty of the state, in spite of the unimpeached authority lost its *de facto* sovereignty. Its failure to fulfil its obligations to the community affected that sovereignty, whether recognized or not, and this serious loss of prestige was never more apparent than when the attempt to suppress the Search by a violent challenge failed.

This failure led actually to some sort of retreat on the part of the state; it could not be otherwise, since violence — as a method — proved to be useless and unavailing compared to the technique of open abstention which the Search professed and followed. The real difference between the two techniques lay in the fact that while abstention was derived from a fresh interpretation of history which was both consistent and comprehensive, violence was but a repetition of an old technique which has never succeeded. It was apparent that the failure of the state, in spite of its supreme position, was due to the simple fact that it was based on an illusory account of the values which history so far embodied.

The most unexpected challenge to the sovereignty of the state by the Search, perhaps, never had its parallel in history. There had been instances in the past in which the community lived without a state (or some institution or other) which kept order and looked to the defence of the community: this happened generally in the short interval between the rout of a state and the occupation of its territory by a ruthless enemy. There had been also cases which came about periodically when considerable portions of the human society were decimated by visitations which either Nature or Providence decreed. But the conditions which followed the failure of the ruling class acting on behalf of the state to disband the Search were unusual and most peculiar. If the Search refused to take the place of the state — there was virtually no state — the community did not suffer; rather it was never in so assured and secure a position as it was after the state had become, to all appearance, defunct. It was never so fully aware of its dignity as now, or so compact and harmonious a body. It was as if the people themselves functioned as the state — they could easily do that if they liked since there was no environment which called for defence. The conditions at the moment almost resembled what the Communist, like many others in human tradition, described as the Golden Age.

But no Golden Age in history, fabulous or historical, lasted for long. It marked only the high watermark of agreement or community of interests as a sign of relief from a long persisting tension. Its quality, again, was wholly emotional, and so it receded as soon as the relief from tension had spent itself. At any rate, no such state in the history of the human community formed the basis of a social scheme.

There was no evidence that the community, after the failure of the ruling class, was a merely emotional body: on the contrary, it was more intent on construction than cultivation of the emotion of relief. What was predominant in its attitude was the eagerness to utilize the new ethics and build the community in all its phases on it so that the tension which warfare, whether violent or non-violent, perpetually created might be avoided once and for ever. No state could any longer mobilize the people for warfare on the plea that there was the Evil across the border to fight. There was no such thing as Evil, but only competing illusions, and the proper course with regard to them was mutual abstention, not warfare.

But how in the midst of all this anomaly did the state actually behave?

The states evidently had reasons to be much more dumbfounded than ever before. And yet by some strange destiny, the ultra-modern one among them seemed to be perfectly confident and fully assured. This state almost devotedly put its faith in what it believed to be Science and seemed to be unusually interested in two things — the production of goods and the suppression of those who stood in the way of their production by competition. Indeed what is called economic interest today christened by Marx as paramount, seemed to be the primary objective of the people of this state. They also talked with full faith about moral purpose and spiritual need, but it is not clear how they could at the same time insist on providing for the economic or material basis as if it were the first and foremost need of man, which is nothing if not Marxism. Yet they honestly looked upon the Marxist as the devil incarnate, the only obstacle in the path of the freedom-loving peoples of the earth. The issue becomes really complicated, as the only original achievement that stands to their credit is exhausted in craftsmanship. The world has yet to learn if they have formulated any new theory even of the physical universe in which they specialize as craftsmen. When they talk about problems of thought or spiritual issues or art and literature they follow scrupulously the model of the classical or modern European from whom their ancestors descended. Even the best of them do not repudiate the idea that Pragmatism, their chief contribution, is philosophy, or that replacing rubber by a synthetic preparation is science, or that repeating the same model time after time is art. And those who are really thoughtful are ashamed of their leadership complex since it derives from mere craftsmanship and nothing more original than that. Finally, at least some frankly look back to their past history and shudder at the thought of the nemesis which, to them, is bound to follow.

It was only natural, therefore, that this state would not accept the review of history which the Search had formulated;

nor could the ethics of abstention possibly be agreeable to their temperament which insists on action to the point of aberration. Instead, the highly placed among them even felt as if the Search was a huge conspiracy to overthrow the science of the modern age and deprive their state of its hard-won position in the community of states. Indeed to them all this was nothing but a trick to cut short the career of imperialism just when this state appeared in the twentieth century to take its share in it. Why should history suddenly stop functioning in the way it had done for at least 6,000 years and when, without any doubt, the time had come for an experiment in neo-European imperialism? Perhaps they were much too obsessed with their industrial efficiency to ask the question whether what they called the usual course of history, at that rate, would ever stop.

In fact, the situation in the twentieth century as it passed the meridian was full of pathos if not quite enigmatic. Or how was it that it should have been left to the least sophisticated state in the Western world to dispose of the fresh verdict on history? If indeed the hour was due for a complete change in the tradition of all history, what could it possibly be that made this young and inexperienced state resist that claim for a radical change?

This was the question which was present to everybody's mind in the Search, and in good time the philosopher, as usual, took it up and made a clean analysis of it.

He made two comments about the people of the new state. They seemed not to have an adequate sense of history or an intimate grasp of tradition as all the old and ancient states, European and Asian, unmistakably had; and they had never in fact had the chance to take part in any of the profound conflicts between the historic civilizations of the human race.

"The truth of this," the philosopher said, "is by no means contradicted by the strenuous efforts the people of the new state have made to study the history of traditions and races ever since they came out of their adolescence and formed a nation — say a couple of centuries ago."

He was only too anxious to recognize that the young intellectuals of this new state were very brilliant indeed, and worked conscientiously under the direct tuition of the most erudite of Europeans. Obviously, their highest ambition had been to be apt pupils of these giants and re-enter through discipleship into the spirit of European civilization. But the result of these honest efforts strangely enough did not make them truly European, not to say sophisticated or profound — and this even though they honestly took the European civilization to be the acme of all civilizations.

> It will be cynicism to ignore the fact that the pious citizens of this state go on a pilgrimage to Rome or Canterbury or Paris as the Mohammedans go to Mecca and the Jews to Palestine, year in and year out. And as if to preserve the rhythm of that life, the intellectuals in their turn earnestly seek light from memories which still, like late autumn, cling to the classical past and breathe with great emotion the air round the ruins of Parthenon or the Academies of Greece; or reproduce the Magdalen Tower of Oxford in the university cities at enormous cost, sometimes in more than one street; or come over regularly to Europe to gaze at ancient buildings to take back home as much inspiration as possible. No pilgrimage was ever more earnest or single-minded: but by some strange cosmic economy, in spite of all their devotion to the still surviving memorials in stone, paint or sound, they have failed, hitherto, to develop the subtle trait of character known as European. They have certainly not become European. What they have become instead is another story. And it may easily shock the anthropologists

> of this new state if one suggested that perhaps they were all the time slowly but steadily yielding to the age-old influences of their own continent and might in course of time even sponsor a revival of the ancient races on whom their own ancestors had fallen in the past like the blazing fire on the prairie. Nature exacts ruthlessly the toll from those who even by mistake cross her path.

"But the claim," the philosopher said, "that they are a new offshoot from the European stock and might any day lay the foundation of another imperial adventure like the one which is just closing down is far-fetched and fantastic. Europe wants rest and not a fresh surge of imperial activity under the aegis of this new state; and, while resting, her dream would be one of peace in the human home, not warfare. She has had quite enough of it."

And here the philosopher made a very illuminating comment on the racial feature of these new people in the Western world. "I feel convinced," he said,

> that the citizens of this new state will never have to repeat in their career the experience of the dread which has filled the European mind, at least since the First World War. The memory of the past of Europe which is responsible for this dread has not been inherited by these new people. In their blood-stream, as our scientist will say, there is no trace of what happened between the modern and the medieval European nor of the bitter conflict between the Christian and the Pagan which closed the Classical period. Nothing of that history has survived as living tradition in the minds of the citizens of this state as they came to form an altogether new racial type. They certainly have not inherited the European's sense of guilt or his sense of supreme merit in the total achievement of that history. Here is a clean departure from the European tradition.
>
> And that is the reason why, today, the verdict on history which the Search has so vividly formulated makes no impression on them. It is difficult not to believe that they

> have no historical sense, in the European or Asian sense of the term. Apparently, the recent verdict on history can be felt or judged only by those who have had a long continuous career in which the pattern of history was variously displayed. No race or civilization, if they had that career, could possibly escape the nemesis which such a pattern implied. Indeed, if by any chance the citizens of this state could feel the dread, as it appears today in Europe — the dread that the Dark Age may come back again and the Far East may cross the seas and take back from Europe all that she ever lost to her — they would have fallen in with the Search at once and recognized the tremendous strength of the new ethics of abstention. As it is, they cannot make head or tail of it.

"If, again, the citizens of this state felt bound to take interest in the affairs of the world, mainly by virtue of their enormous resources in men and materials and a new technique of exploiting them," the philosopher continued, "it still would not follow that they would not approach the affairs of the world in a doctrinaire spirit. On the contrary, the means of relief they have already suggested seem to be, in the last analysis, academic and unrealistic. Possibly because they have no grasp of the inwardness of the cultures which are different from — or even opposed to — what they call their own they could only precipitate conflicts and warfare in spite of their honest intention to help. Technically they have no real sense of the dialectic of history, and one of the ironies of our age is that a modest political view, now completely outmoded, should have taken the proportion of a creed with them. The irony consists in nothing so much as in the fact that the meteoric success of sheer economic achievement was preceded by what many of their own authorities call by the name of ruthless exploitation of men, animals and soil on a continental scale. It is difficult, indeed, after such 'achievement', to follow the design and course of history, if one still has to think of a merciful God and beneficent Law."

10

At this stage of the talk suddenly a question was put to the philosopher. "Does it follow then that sooner or later this new state is bound to come into clash with the Search in the shape, say, of a siege which the diehards of the new state may stage?"

"The issue," the philosopher remarked at once,

> is no longer one of prospecting the nature of conflict, but of assessing the exact place of the new state in the background of the drama which the twentieth century has so unmistakably staged. What part are these new people expected to play in the outstanding split between the East and the West? That is the only test by which their merit as a nation can be judged.
>
> Can it be argued that this new state is in a position to arbitrate between Europe and Asia, between West and East? Is there any evidence that the main clash between the two social schemes — group and individualist — can be judged and tested in the light of what the new people uphold as the only legitimate and adequate form of that state? Even if one accepts their bona fides when the democratic state is held up by them as the panacea for all evils, would that concession make any difference to the split between the East and the West? It would be unpardonable to forget that the main issue between Asia and Europe today is not one of autocracy or democracy: the democratic state is no more relevant than the autocratic. The issue today is one of clash

between the ultimate social schemes, both of which embody autocracy and democracy as mere techniques for realizing their objectives. Even if one grants that the new state has deployed its democratic framework so ingeniously as to build up economic pre-eminence within a short span of years, even such a phenomenon only repeats a stage of European history which is just disappearing. Political ascendancy and economic paramountcy, whatever their scale, are not exactly the means to employ to solve the issue between ultimate social schemes. If indeed the merciful God of the new state gave them a bountiful continent and an urge to exploit it till a new technique of production replaced all others of old — the same thing happened many a time, even in the animal world — that cannot mean that they were at once qualified to arbitrate between the ancient and classical civilizations of the East and the West. The issue between the East and the West is not one of production or distribution according to a standard or plan which the democratic state of the new people rigidly lays down. The issue is one of laying down the very structure of the society of man and that on a completely fresh pattern.

The new technique of production or craftsmanship may still claim for the moment to rejuvenate the West and even to halt the imperialist in his retreat. There may in consequence be the shadow of an attempt to restore Western dominion over the whole of the earth's surface. Whilst these possibilities cannot be wholly ruled out even such a shadow could only be restless and brief. Nothing indeed can put the split between the East and the West into abeyance once it has arisen: the only alternative to the split is resolution. Every European knows that; and there is not one among them who will choose freely the revival of imperialism even if it be guaranteed by patronage or by some temporary device. The dread I have referred to is much too intense and deep in the European mind to be dispelled by the prospects which a mere technique of production may raise. That continent today is much too wide awake to be persuaded by a mere diversion.

Still, the European may willingly accept help from this new race for his preservation, and may even claim that help — on the ground that as an offshoot from the European stock it is the duty of the new people to keep the European peoples well fed and well housed as a matter of elementary manners. Perhaps a small minority may even dream of restoring the imperial eminence of the European by a judicious exploitation of the new people's resources. But no true scion of Europe could for a moment believe that the new people, by their merely technical progress, could be capable of taking a leading part in the main drama between the East and the West. That, at least, is the European view, if we trace it to its roots.

Besides, the question of mediation between the East and the West by this new state does not actually arise: these new people are already involved in a terrific clash with the Communist state, which in some sense belongs to the East. Indeed, if one judges the leaders of the new state by the way they talk, they must somehow have found in the Communist state the Evil Incarnate — and naturally feel in duty bound to destroy it. How could it be possible for the new state in such a situation to arbitrate between the East and the West?

It is another issue whether it is at all relevant to waste any state's energy in fighting communism at this late hour. The fact is that since the split between the East and the West has arisen the very idea of a conflict between communism and capitalism has automatically died a natural death. Neither the socialist nor the capitalist now can count upon a long lease of life, since they are not the real figures on the stage today. In fact, all internal conflicts, whether in the Eastern or in the Western social schemes, have truly become irrelevant. Neither the West nor the East can afford any longer to fight for democracy or autocracy, since the whole of the individualistic scheme of the West has been challenged by the group scheme of the East.

If in spite of all these obvious facts a challenge does actually come to the Search from the new people, one thing is certain — it will instantly provoke a war between them and the Eastern states. Would the new people then offer such a challenge and provoke such a war? One obvious answer is that a good many of them have for long been impatient to start it. But the fact equally is that beyond making preparation for such a war — and that on as huge a scale as possible — the Eastern states have been scrupulously left alone by them. What could be the reason of this strange holding back in the face of all the impatience? Why in any case all this unnecessary waste of energy?

There is a very important question to answer if we want to get down to the bottom of this strange fact of restraining impatience. Would the new state be allowed by its allies in Europe to provoke a war with the Eastern states, whatever the chances of success? The answer is clearly in the negative, since it is the Europeans rather than the Eastern states who run the risk of being completely disintegrated by such a fateful war if it were to come. However strange it may sound, nothing is more plain to the European than that the new people are totally incapable of visualizing the consequences of such a war — incapable also of seeing that such virile, earnest people as the communists, who successfully staged a revolution, could not be expected gracefully to spare the Europeans if they got seriously tied up with the new people. If the fates willed that the communists were to lose the reward of their revolution and be turned back from the gates of Heaven, the same fate would see to it that at any rate Europe would be reduced to a shambles by them and the new people left to spend the rest of their life in monastic atonement.

Perhaps not even the new people are quite unfamiliar with the grim prospects of an atomic war. One should not miss the fact that they themselves feel as insecure in their own home as the Europeans or any other people in theirs, whatever the deep-lying causes for this. If they do not suffer from the historic European sense of dread there might easily be some corresponding sense of guilt in them — to be traced necessarily to what they in their past must have committed when they ruthlessly destroyed the indigenous civilizations of their new continent for the noble purpose of establishing themselves in it. If suppressions of cultures and races have been inevitable in history, the nemesis that followed them sooner or later was equally inevitable: no reasons ever given for such suppressions could cheat it of its even flow.

If there is no legitimate ground for holding that the new people would offer a challenge to the Search, for the simple reason that such a step would be sure to lead to their desertion by their European allies and to the grim prospect of being completely isolated, does it not follow that they have, at least, to take the Search as a genuine phenomenon? At any rate it should on no account be completely ignored, since it is steadily depleting the manpower and moral support on which the new people, too, have to depend for sheer existence. No state can rule or govern if there is no community to govern. Besides, the European community has been won over to the Search in principle and the community of the new state, too, may choose any day to follow the Search and its European supporters rather than their own political leadership. It is perfectly arguable that if the states in Europe have lost the support of their communities, the state of the new people may lose the allegiance of its community also, sooner or later.

The obvious feature of the situation in Europe today is that in the very heart of it there is definitely what appears to be a paradox. As a community Europe is practically existing in a stateless condition, and yet not one of her states has either disappeared or been superseded by a completely new formation. It would be a mistake to assert that the European communities are being ruled or governed at the moment by

> the state, as they used to be: and yet not a single community has deserted its own state and gone over to its opposite number. The main reason why such an unusual situation has arisen is that no conflict seems any longer to exist either for the community or for the state. In so far as the community has accepted the ethics of mutual abstention which the Search has formulated, it has come right out of the vortex of warfare. There is in consequence no longer any need for the state, which specializes in warfare and defence; and the Search in these conditions can well afford to carry on without building up a fresh formation in the light of the ethics of mutual abstention. Yet this functionless state goes on existing as it ever did: herein lies the paradox.
>
> There are still, however, people who plead on behalf of the state and these people openly hold that the state has not only done its part but has done it at enormous sacrifice. If, indeed, it could not keep its promises to the letter, such a failure did not result from any fault of the state but from sheer destiny and fate. No institution could have done any better in its place.

This argument appealed to at least some sections of the community, especially those who had the largest share of the opportunities in life which the state as a machine directly or indirectly controlled. Strangely enough it was on the minds of this section more than on any other that the past, as history recorded it, had a very stronghold. Their argument was that if life has unmistakably been full of ups and downs there was no reason why we should at all try to initiate a change in its course: nobody could claim that life ended in extinction as a result of those ups and downs. Besides it is precisely this alternate rise and fall that is called justice by our philosophers — perhaps the only moral value hitherto recognized. What, then, was wrong with the state? Why look for a change?

It was, of course, normally on this section of the community that the state built its hopes of restoring its power. And evidently the state seemed to be fully assured that the new faith professed by the community was by no means invulnerable: in fact it could be crushed if only the community were cajoled and frightened in turn. After all the sense of fear is not quite dead even in the most advanced people of the human race; and is not that sufficient evidence that sense of gain and attachment to the good things of life must be still prevailing there, too? Why not, then, work on both these weaknesses as of old and alienate the people from the Search? This simple and straightforward scheme should not be difficult to achieve, since the state of the new people has vast resources, which could be drawn upon both for satisfying the sense of gain and striking terror into the heart of the misguided communities.

This, however, did not mean that an alliance between the old historical states and the state of the new people in the interest of a revival of political authority should necessarily be credited with a machiavellian motive; the alliance could be perfectly normal and honest. After all, neither the state nor the people ever play a part which history does not determine. In any case the fact is that the states as a body had had a sudden inspiration about warfare and a rejuvenation of faith in their authority as states. They felt they could not possibly dismantle such a central organization of human society as the state. That would be committing sin against the law of God. It was inconceivable that they should leave the community to the tender mercies of a new-fangled ethics which was meaningless to them. And it made no difference if the Search had the support of a mystical vision. Let the Eastern people, if they like, carry on with such visions as they had done for long centuries. The West had always had a clearer and more rational record and the states as a body would stick to their own tradition.

But as luck would have it the states in alliance to regain their authority counted their prospects without taking into consideration the outstanding feature of the twentieth-century situation. Soon the sense of dread returned and hung like the sword of Damocles.

It is the historian who must be called upon to diagnose the deeper ground for such a fateful oversight on the part of the states. The obvious explanation was the recent, unparalleled success of the neo-European state in tapping the capacity of modern science — in the milieu of unlimited raw materials and of labour supplied by non-European races. It was, perhaps, the same old story of the real situation being suddenly hidden from view by disproportionate success in some isolated spheres of life. The historian generally traces such oversights to short-range calculations, induced by the appalling prospects of long-range ones. But this is by no means a complete explanation — we have to go to the trend of history to discover the deeper grounds. We cannot discuss that trend at this moment.

Whatever the grounds, it was apparent that even the partial success of an attack on the communities, open or veiled, would be sure to be neutralized by two events which would inevitably follow: the immediate return of the dread and the steady rise of an alliance between the communities of Europe and the Eastern states. The dread would descend inevitably from the trend of history and paralyse the states as a body; and it would not be long before the spectre of devastation by the atom bomb would pursue them with relentless hate. Soon, perhaps very soon, even a split would follow between the new state and the community which it ruled. And then an alliance between the communities of the new and old states would arise, exactly as the alliance between the states had arisen. The result would be complete isolation of the state and its inevitable consequence, the breakdown of the alliance between the states.

The philosopher took great care to point out that these two alliances — that between the states and that between the communities — should not be confused with the familiar alliances of history between what is known as the right and left wings.

The issue between the competing alliances, he repeated, was not one of freedom on the one side and order on the other, between democracy and autocracy. The issue definitely was one of survival for both the state and the community. It had to be discovered what change in the constitution of the state and in the organization of the community would preserve them both after they had abjured autocratic and democratic ideas and values. If both the state and the community had to live by the ethics of mutual abstention and not by the traditional methods of violence and persuasion, what radical changes would have to be introduced into the respective forms of their groupings?

11

The whole Meeting was urged by the philosopher to note the extreme importance of these changes. And he also emphasized that in no sense was the twentieth century like any other century on record, even if we concede to all the centuries of the past the scale and proportion of an epoch.

> The truth is that the twentieth century has, after untold frustrations in the shape of alternate warfare and compromise, at last succeeded in formulating a true resolution of the most baffling antinomies in human experience. It should be possible now to formulate a new organization of its constitution in order to save human history from repeating the conflicts of old.
>
> Only the other day there was the memorable frustration of half-a-century's effort in a concentrated form to realize the doctrine of love. Such an effort was never known before as far back as one might go, as evidently it could not be. The frustration took place in broad daylight and yet not even an apology was rendered by the fearless, selfless opponent who was responsible for this frustration. But what followed was not the rise of the doctrine of warfare, but just the routine execution of that opponent of the doctrine of love by the state which mourned the death of love. The total loss of life was two instead of one; and it almost seemed as if no life was left. But it was not all tragedy. A third event happened in the same universe which staged the dual tragedy and

> this marked a resolution of the clash between the doctrine of love and its direct opposite, the doctrine of warfare.

It is this resolution of the conflict between incompatibles which has been long overdue in human history, and the case for it was put before the meeting with great earnestness by the philosopher. Indisputably, he pointed out, there was now a way of disposing of conflict without warfare, violent or non-violent. What, therefore, was almost a riddle to him was that even the historic states in the West should still be impervious to this fact. It was most unintelligible that, while the communities under the guidance of the Search should have accepted this new way, the states which claimed to be their guardian should still be trying hard to frustrate them and revive the method of warfare — and that, strangely enough, in the interests of peace.

He added:

> It is quite another issue, however, what exactly is going to happen in the near future. There may even be some fresh attempt to precipitate at least some kind of warfare by the state of the new people. And this may happen for one or more reasons. As I have already said, this state — being young — has no adequate historical sense, as both the European and the Asian states certainly have. It seems to be totally unaware of the fact that history stages conflict between social systems just as much as it stages conflict between democracy and autocracy, which are but techniques in those systems. History has so far only recorded the conflict between techniques.
>
> And so, most unfortunately, the young state has altogether missed the fact that conflicts which lie between the two conceptions of autocracy and democracy are no longer the real conflict today. And this fact, if by any chance it is presented to that state, appears to be not only meaningless but offensive. It is still thinking in all good faith and with

> honest conviction that democracy, as understood by it, is Peace or perhaps the Divine on earth.
>
> Finally, the new state is completely ignorant of or perhaps oblivious of the fact that there are only two alternatives present before the Western world today — either it will have to submit to the East in exactly the same way as the East had to submit to the West during the last two to three centuries (the new state will fall, with Europe, precipitately if it is involved with the West in reviving the imperial past): or a fresh social scheme will be developed which will rule out all warfare and provide for the mutual existence on equal terms of both the East and the West. (The new state will have a golden opportunity to survive and construct if that happens.)

"It is painful to me to think," the philosopher said, "that the old and historic states, under the impulsive pressure from the state of the new people, might be led to precipitate the first alternative. The fact is that the new state is incapable of thinking that the dread in the European mind is not an idle wind but is rooted in the trend of European history. That history covers both the medieval civilization of Europe and the mystical civilization of Asia. It will be a misfortune in the history of the human race if they do succeed in deadening the European mind. Fortunately, however, the signs on the horizon," the philosopher contended, "perhaps do not indicate any such Nemesis. They rather imply, if we look closely, that a split in the alliance between the states will arise to avert such a misfortune. And then the state in the New World will either capitulate to the Search or live for a time completely isolated on its own continent at the mercy of its past."

There is in the archives of Europe no record of events from which one could gather what exactly happened in the Western world after the philosopher had so prophetically read the signs on the horizon. But there is ample evidence that none of the three which played such prominent parts in the twentieth-century drama disappeared from view: the Search, the states and the communities continued to function as if they could live together if not in amity, at least without hostility.

There was, however, a great change in the non-European world. The East was taking off the loads from her back and trying to stand upright and erect and so the split between the East and the West was steadily growing to its true proportion. And this meant anxious efforts in the old states to prevent this change if possible, especially as the state of the new people, since it had its own idea of perpetuating the Western leadership of the world, was only too prone to underwrite such efforts.

The European mind, if we trace its roots to where the instincts most relentlessly rule, was occupied, however, with grave concern about the split between the East and the West and the persistent dread that this implied. To assess the significance of what was happening, therefore, one has to leave the minor, subsidiary events and concentrate on the relations between the Search, the states and the communities in the Western world at the moment.

Fortunately we have a very vivid account of this period from a Chinese historian who stood detached from the main split between the East and the West, and in this account the historian measured the bearing of the Western world in the midst of the changes which were rapidly taking place. It was brought to the Search by the historian himself and it read, exactly as all classical Chinese accounts do, as a truly objective picture without a shred, of the personal stimulating its theme. What was evident was that this great historian somehow managed to enter into the body and spirit of the Western people in the middle of the twentieth century before producing an account of their mode of existence at the time. And this is by no means a fantastic comment to make, since it is well known that no Chinese artist of the true classical type would dare, for instance, to paint a bird singing in the bamboo grove with the myriad leaves keeping the song to its rhythm without first translating himself bodily into that grove.

His account was that the Search, the state and the community all lived side by side without any sign of a clash or conflict between them. There was no war in the Western world, nor any instance of a serious disturbance in the domestic concerns of the people who lived on that continent. But the states did not accept the ethics of mutual abstention which both the Search and the community upheld, while the latter discarded the ethics of warfare to which the states were committed by law, whatever the source.

But as there was no open conflict, the administration of the common interests of the people was carried on as smoothly as possible. At least the needs of the people which were essential were fully met and the people in their turn made no demands which could be easily opposed by contrary claims. In fact, as the state went on meeting the common needs of the people, the people went on working for the state.

As the historian was gently relating this account, the philosopher asked leave to put a few questions to get at the implications of his most valuable statement.

> Does the historian mean that the old and historic states are not following any particular line of administration but just ensuring that the main interests of the people, which are common and unambiguous, are fully met? Would it then be a mistake to call the old states either by the name of democratic or autocratic which all states have so far invariably been?

The answer was to the point, as all Chinese answers are. "I

am not an authority on these very complicated notions of autocracy and democracy," the historian begged the Meeting to remember.

> I really get confused when I come across these two notions in all parts of the world, since they change colour like the chameleon. When, for instance, the state across the Atlantic calls democracy another name for peace, it seems to me that peace means war. But when I find that a state on the Indian ocean, at the foot of the Himalayas, calls democracy by the name of peace, I have to turn a somersault in the inner chamber of my thought and call peace by its real name. Similarly, the notion of autocracy has equally developed many and varied meanings. The House of God in all traditions was taken as the supreme seat of all autocracy — but the universal claim on its behalf by those who spoke in His name has been that it was the only institution which guaranteed freedom to the individual. Naturally, when I speak to assemblies of learned men and women I speak with great diffidence. I cannot use all the meanings at once since I am not lecturing to students to create a vacuum in their minds. If the philosopher assures me that he will be kind and forgive my incompetence, I shall just state what I think is the proper answer to his very valuable questions.
>
> The point that I wanted to emphasize was that there was no sign of a dual interest in the European world when I visited it and therefore it would not be right to call the state either democratic or autocratic, since I found out from my long experience of history that the terms democracy and autocracy implied one another. There was no doubt a state at the time I had the privilege of visiting Europe, but nobody raised the issue either of freedom or unity. And what was most unusual was that the state was never called upon to preserve order. How this happened I could not tell, but the situation reminded me of a saying of one of our logicians: "If there was one thing, and then another thing, it would

> follow at once that there would be a 'third thing'. Perhaps, I thought, the European state was, by now, somehow led to deal with that 'third thing' and completely relieved of its usual predilection to deal with the first at the expense of the second and then to change over to the second to the detriment of the first. It was a phenomenal discovery to me since I was never taught even by Confucius that the European could by any chance be led to value the 'third thing'."

The whole meeting was greatly impressed and all the members rose to their feet to thank their noble guest. Such a reception was the more embarrassing to him since he felt that it came straight from the very heart of the members. The philosopher now explained to the historian what the Search stood for in their ethics of mutual abstention, and how that ethics — while in practice negating the conflict between democracy and autocracy — emphasized the central significance of the ideal of a community, which means the common interest. If therefore the Western world did exist in a form in which only the common interest was to be realized, it should not be at all extravagant to hope that the states might see the possibility of abstaining from the interests which are in conflict by reason of their incompatibility. Where then would the claim for warfare stand?

The Search now wanted to do honour to this distinguished visitor from the East and in the highly approved style of hospitality of the Western world, a banquet was prepared. In the meantime a tea was arranged by the members who were most anxious to meet him and all the leading minds came to it. There was, however, a little confusion in the Committee which was asked to organize the tea and the confusion arose on the issue whether the "pure green blades of a most unearthly grass" from China or what is called "tea" in the land of the Buddha should be served for him. And this difficulty was preceded by a debate on the classical problem whether the

Chinese scholars of Taoism, sensing the advent of the Buddha, sent over this "unearthly grass" to his land to refresh him immediately after his birth or whether the countrymen of the Great Gautama came over to fetch the grass from China for the Chinese tribute for that anticipated birth. No conclusion was reached but some drink was served which goes by the name of tea in Europe. Perhaps that was the solution!

There was a lot of talk about Confucius, Lao-tze and Buddha and the general opinion was that all these three, if they were alive today, would be in perfect agreement with the ethics of mutual abstention. The historian himself fully endorsed the view and suggested that behind this twentieth-century formulation one could somehow sense the noble spirit of those divine sages actually operating. The Chinese mind did not want war; it was essentially and integrally peaceful, as was the mind which appeared in the land of Gautama the Buddha. In a very graceful way he said:

> Just as the Great Dragon that was painted by the greatest artist of the time for the joy of the Emperor flew away through the hidden aperture in the ceiling the moment he was given the last touch to his eyes, the codes which Confucius, Lao-tze and Buddha left behind became truly alive as soon as the ethics of mutual abstention lifted the mantle which covered them.

12

It was not long after this remarkable testimony from a Chinese to the harmonious working between the state, the community and the Search when the sophisticated groups of men and women suggested to the leaders of the Search that the Conference which the states had organized should be revived. If it had been possible for all the three sections of the European society to work at all together without in any way coming into clash, why should not this very fact be made the basis for a fresh investigation both of the causes of the differences between them and of the way to a resolution of these differences? If neither warfare nor internal conflict were necessary for their mutual existence, should not the Search, whose ideal was Truth, approach the states to come to the Conference and examine the problems again? And this time some at least of the Eastern states might be approached to join the Western states.

The suggestion was received very cordially by the whole Search. It did not appear to anybody that the states might take offence or suspect the move as a strategic one to undermine their prestige. In any case it was open to the states to reject the proposal. In the last analysis, it all depended on the common interest, if there was such a thing, binding the Search and the states together.

And it seemed that there was in fact such a common meeting ground. If the community did not revolt against the states in spite of the sharp differences between them, and if the Search did not in any way question the right of the states to govern, there must be a reason for this strange situation. Evidently, the community and the Search did not believe that there was any longer any occasion for warfare: and the states were convinced that warfare was irrelevant to the present situation since the people of the Search and the community could not be coerced by them to join it. As the Chinese historian had said, the state, the Search and the community had actually lived together and fulfilled their respective obligations in working out the essential interests. Alliance between the states, again, was a thing of the past and war on a large scale was inconceivable for at least two continuing reasons: the presence of the dread, which neutralized faith in success, and the replacement of conflict as between democracy and autocracy by clash between social systems.

What could be the difficulties, then, which might still prevent the states from meeting the Search and the community at a Conference? If there was any ground still left for reinstating the past order of society as it existed even at the beginning of the Second World War, the Conference would be totally irrelevant and uncalled for. But history is not exactly a creation of the Western mind. On the contrary the note struck in recent years, which has been ringing now for some time in every European mind, refers to the steady decline of the European Age and not to a resurgence of its past imperial glory. Not even scientific miracles, whatever their proportion, can deaden that note. There is nothing left over in the Western world after the two wars and the two dreams which can even hypnotize the European mind to believe that it can get rid of its dread. And the state of the new people is perhaps in a worse condition, since it lacks the sense of history in its true proportion and seems to have been carried away by modern science as if it rested on a stable view of the physical universe: a misfortune which has happened to them when the whole basis of science — on which it has hitherto flourished — is, like the granite bed of the earth in the dream, cracking up. No scientist, any more than any philosopher or mathematician, has yet succeeded in solving the problem of organization. And until that solution has arrived the successes of science are as much at the mercy of events as hitherto all philosophic and mathematical contributions have been. There is no tradition in which the two incompatible factors of unity and individuality, the prime essentials of all organization have been equally provided for: so no organization has hitherto been anything but a device. Apparently leadership today is bound up with that achievement and nothing short of it. It is not synthetic rubber or the atom bomb that can guarantee such a claim: such things will soon be superseded, as such claims have been in all history.

But the air was still shrouded in fog so far as the prospects of an immediate Conference were concerned. The states were not in the mood yet to say good-bye to tradition and the Search was apparently rather disinclined to take the initiative.

Before any serious attempt could be made even to come to a decision, a whole deputation came over from the Far East to discuss some very serious issues with the Search. They had heard about it from many quarters and the impression which people all over the world had formed about it was that it had got, as by a miracle, the key to the complete resolution of conflict. To them that key was the most immediate need of the human race, since modern science has left it completely at the mercy of the so-called physical universe. Perhaps the universe, as a whole, was never truly known by any tradition on record; and so, necessarily, no God or Truth or Beauty was ever wholly what they had been claimed to be. And yet, what was most strange, the blunders of tradition did not precipitate a wreckage of the universe, as if to prove to the sceptic that he was hopelessly mistaken. Only modern science wanted to go one better and, today, as a direct result of its contribution we have suddenly become a beneficiary perhaps of eternal rest in the lap of death. Indeed there was nothing in the archives of tradition to challenge this sudden coup by the scientist, since nobody really knew either what conflict meant or how it could be resolved. It was not even known that the crux of the whole situation lay in the view held about conflict. If conflict did after all mean only negation and destruction and nothing else, if impasse or confusion was the only possible finale to it, modern science is right and all other wisdom is wrong.

The deputation, with great humility, put their case before the Search. The men and women who came with the deputation did not come from the heart of the ascetic East or from the intelligentsia brought up on Western lore: but they were in direct touch with them both and above all felt that they were pre-eminently Eastern in their outlook and temperament. In any case they unmistakably claimed unity and peace as the goal or gospel of the East.

It was not, however, possible for them, they frankly said, to uphold the interpretation of unity so far known in the Eastern tradition. They had practically no alternative to questioning all the interpretations of history hitherto known and that, for two reasons: these interpretations did not prevent perpetual warfare, and did not even explain why warfare, since it was a fact, was indispensable to the universe. In fact, in their opinion, the notion of peace in tradition was indistinguishable from warfare, if one looked closely into its meaning.

Could the Search suggest to them a fresh interpretation of unity and peace and also account for the grim history we have had to go through?

It gave the philosopher a fresh opportunity to expound the main position of the Search with special reference to the interpretation of history and to the ethics of mutual abstention that followed from it. The issue which came to be discussed at length, however, centred in the notion of justice since it had a direct bearing on the main trend of thought and feeling in the Western world at the moment. If justice was the keynote of history, if it guaranteed to both sides in a conflict the same chances of defeat and victory, did it not follow that the last three centuries of European domination must necessarily be followed by at least an equal period of European suppression? At any rate the persistent dread in the European mind points to such a possibility. And perhaps as long as this dread remained the states would find it difficult to abandon their method of warfare. The most peculiar position in the Western world today was that, while the dread — by inducing a lack of faith — kept the states as a body from precipitating a "hot war", it was also instrumental in keeping them from accepting the ethics of mutual abstention . . . as if there was some reason somewhere why Justice should not literally prevail at this late hour!

The philosopher made this point with great urgency to the deputation and asked for a comment. Did the Eastern people really and truly demand justice? Did they, in other words, expect that the Western world would have to go through the same kind of suppression at the hands of the Eastern states as the latter had had to go through at the hands of the West only the other day? Was that necessity what they would call equalization by the Law of *karma*? And did it mean in their language the provision for true democracy in history or democracy as worked out in the Cosmic scheme?

The reply came instantly:

> If the doctrine of unity which is the main ideal of the East meant Peace, the Law of *karma* or *dharma* which does mean justice, or "Cosmic democracy", as it may be called, could not have implied perpetual and never-ending warfare. So long as warfare was inevitable it had to be subject to the Law of *karma,* since otherwise there would be no justice or equalization. But the Law of *karma* is not the universe, it presupposes the universe. And why should the universe provide only for war or the Law of *karma* and not also for harmony — or for quite another law which may go with harmony? The truth in the heart of the East pointed to a conclusion which was against the universality of the Law of *karma.* Even the interpretation of unity, whether as *atman* or *nirvana,* makes no room for any such universality.
>
> No Asian would today demand justice for its own sake provided it was possible to guarantee harmony. If, however, harmony was ruled out by the universe altogether the law of *karma* would inexorably prevail and justice would be the standard of Cosmic value. That is the Eastern view.
>
> Our submission to the Search is that the issue is no longer one of justice or Law of *karma* or Law of Causation if we go by the need of the human mind in the twentieth century. The issue is one of discovering a way out of conflict different from the way of warfare; to which all states as a matter of necessity have been committed, whether in a violent or non-violent form, since the beginning of history. And it is for a resolution of this issue that we have come to the distinguished body of the Search.

The reply was given by the philosopher after he had, on behalf of the Search, expressed deep gratitude for being so firmly assured as to what the East was thinking, and how it saw the implications of the dread in the European mind. It was a great relief to the Search to be told that the period of justice for the sake of justice was over, even if one could not make a statistical review of its proportion in human history. The Search was also grateful to learn that at least the most representative and deep-seated feeling in the East today was looking for harmony — not mere justice. It was great good news that the Eastern peoples would much rather forgo their dues from the West as assessed by the historian, and have harmony instead.

The philosopher once again referred to his analysis of history, to the ethics of mutual abstention and to the possibility of building up a common home for the human species with one type of state which would organize and administer the human family.

His reply was given the warmest reception possible by a large group of earnest men and women who had come as visitors to the meeting, who found in the opinion of the deputation from the East almost the fulfilment of what they had been looking for as a result of their long investigation into the wisdom of the East.

It is now some centuries since this remarkable investigation was started and the motives that inspired it at its inception were by some mischance varied and diverse: and so it happened that it was periodically held up either by a complete lack of understanding or by the strong mutual suspicion prevailing between the East and the West. In the language of the historian, it was the dialectic of history that rigidly shaped its course. If the East and the West failed to see eye to eye on any issue by reason of some innate incompatibility between them, it was not possible that investigation, however well-intentioned, to unravel the exact relationship between them would fare well. Indeed, it actually led to many an unfortunate incident in which truth came to be distorted either as a matter of choice or simply from necessity. Even traditions gradually arose with apparently no other purpose than that of vilifying the character of the two civilizations by wilful misrepresentation of facts. And it was on the basis of such traditions that romances were built up in sheer political and cultural conceit to wound deliberately the susceptibilities of the peoples concerned. What followed necessarily was the deepening of the conflict between the two hemispheres, which gave birth to actual harm to both, to a degree perhaps impossible to measure. And when on top of this the cynics on both sides proposed apologies by tracing the differences to mere racial idiosyncrasies, they only added insult to injury.

All this storm and stress in due course gradually yielded, however, to the main trend of history and the stage for romance had to be dismantled as history dictated. And then one had to reckon with the verdict of time, which unmistakably pointed to the relativity of values and the utter falsity of absolute claims. The stand for values and standards had to be abandoned and gradually it became clear that there was no special virtue in sharing gospels or not sharing them, in building fortresses or not building them, or in producing goods and manufacturing weapons or not producing or manufacturing them. It was soon seen that neither side produced any result on which one could count, except for a periodic sense of vigour and self-glorification, inevitably followed by acute depression. At least the deeper minds realized that what was writ large on the face of all history was complete frustration as the final state. As the artist might put it, the main motif of all history was to produce just the anguish of soul which stands symbolized in the slow, unsteady march back to an empty home from the ever-recurring funeral on the banks of the Ganges or on the hilltop or in the highly decorated cemetery.

This was the account of the long investigation by the Western world into the wisdom of the East; and while the earnest group of visitors endorsed it, their leaders accepted with joy the conclusion which the deputation from the Eastern people put before the meeting. They said:

> Indeed the East has ever been truly anxious for the discovery of Truth — and by that she never failed to mean unity. If, still, justice or the Law of *karma* is the ruling factor of history, the East does not want to stay in history but to pass rapidly through its folds.

To this opinion the orientalists, theosophists and missionaries, and some noted administrators who were at the meeting gave wholehearted support. They all agreed that the Eastern mind wanted unity and that justice was but a passing phase, which was perhaps a riddle to them.

> Is it still possible for the states, the seats of learning and the churches to hang back from the Search? Could tradition still demand their allegiance, in the interest of human values? Has the universe still to stage some more acts of the drama of discipline before dismantling that stage for good?

This question seemed to be echoing in everybody's mind and it was soon picked up by the philosopher for analysis. He said:

> One of the most perplexing questions of history has always referred to the lease of life which the drama of discipline, by a Cosmic provision, enjoyed. It has been impossible to calculate the span of the life of illusion. If all the states of the Western world hang back, contrary to all reason, and do not join the Search nothing more can be said about it. There is no force or authority in thought or inspiration to coerce action on any scale. Action goes its own way except when its mainsprings periodically get rusted; and then thought has to remove the doubt — which is sure to prevail — before

action can begin again. It is for the states to decide how they will act and when.

One thing is clear enough, however; and that is that the drama of discipline or illusion cannot maintain itself very much longer on the basis on which it has stood so far. The ground beneath its feet is gone, and by all the evidence it seems to be perfectly arguable that the states will be dismantled. But will they dismantle themselves, since nobody else has a right even to initiate a movement that may lead to that supreme act of self-immolation?

That is just the question. It is for the states to answer. It may well be that the states themselves know that changes are due: they may at this very moment be actually facing the absolute necessity of building the new basis, since it is for them alone to build it. Once Truth has appeared it is inevitable that it will have its way. May we not suppose that the states really are looking for the architect?

It seems inconceivable that the age of warfare could for any length of time survive after it has been seen somewhere in human society that there is another way of dealing with conflict. Such a situation never arose in the past and will not have to arise again in the future since it has already arisen today. Why should one think that the states may still postpone the coming of the new age as a matter of sheer obstinate will?

13

Somehow, at this stage, some of the younger generation of the ruling clique managed to gatecrash the Meeting, which was meant to wind up the long series of meetings of the year. These young men had the firm conviction that the state could and should continue to rule. They felt, moreover, that it was their primary duty to make the state live up to its past. In any case, there was no reason why they themselves should be robbed of the chances which their fathers, grandfathers and great-grandfathers as a matter of prescriptive right enjoyed. Why indeed should they, the descendants of the race of great rulers, soldiers, financiers and industrialists have to disappear like the mist? Was it right that they should be made to work, alongside men and women whose ancestors were for long centuries ruled by theirs? The art of ruling, fighting or administering is, by common consent, a specialized art which took centuries to evolve. If every man and woman is not born as a poet or a painter, it is even more true that very few are born to be ruler, soldier or administrator. The energy and sacrifice needed for running a state or for waging a war on the field of battle or for organizing the varied and complicated interests in the human home are very rare indeed. Why should then this body of specialists be thoughtlessly sacrificed for the sake of a mere theory which is known by the name of the ethics of mutual abstention? Can a theory match the equipment of a ruler who governs or of a soldier who fights? Of what good is a theory to a state if it has not got the weapons with which to fight or the mechanized implements or tools with which to produce or a sufficient number of men and women who will work these weapons or tools? It is ridiculous indeed to think that a state with a fine army, navy and air force should capitulate to a body like the Search, whose only means of defence or construction is just a theory of ethics. Does ethics fight back an enemy, not to speak of initiating a fight with him? Did anybody ever see a moral theory stand up on the field of battle and put up a fight against a hostile force?

It was very difficult indeed for the leaders of the Search to give a reply to these descendants of the ruling clique which would or could meet their immediate need. They were young and evidently had seen only certain phases of life, since they had been indoctrinated by their elders purposefully with half-truths or samples of history taken bodily out of their contexts. There had been no alternative to such a procedure on the part of those elders because they had felt in duty bound to protect their social order at any cost against the challenge which was rapidly increasing from their age-old antagonist. It would be no good raising the deeper issues of history with these young people or discussing a new interpretation of it or suggesting to them that no state stood with its equipment alone but had what it took to be a granite basis of ideals and objectives. They would not see if they were told that the equipment would be useless and completely unavailing if the ideas on which the state rested had not the strength to meet the opposition.

It so happened, however, that the young gatecrashers felt subdued by the very bearing of the learned assembly as soon as they came into direct contact with it. They felt they must respect it and were even in a mood to listen to an analysis of the situation, about which they felt completely desperate. What struck them most was that no case was made for their opponents: the part that their predecessors played was appreciated no more and no less than the part the antagonists of their ancestors had played within the same horizons. And the total comment that was made was that there was nothing in history which could really satisfy the young minds of the twentieth century. They learned from this assembly that there has been a ruling clique who made a claim on behalf of their ancestors throughout history — and that in their own interests when the situation at intervals became desperate. And if by any chance the present assembly did not see any prospect of a change in the rhythm of history, it would have stepped aside and let the state and its opponents carry on as usual. But since the assembly had seen that the rhythm of history was on the verge of a new birth it had no alternative but to stand right out against the method of warfare. The young people were asked to ponder deeply whether their ancestors would not have been really satisfied if they could have achieved their ends by some other method than warfare or if they could have reached permanent peace. In any case it was now too late for any section of the human community to try to stop this new rhythm of history.

It was a different issue whether a bare theory of ethics as soon as formulated could instantly be followed by the building up of a structure of society which alone could embody it in action. Certainly a theory cannot fight on the field of battle or work in a factory or even pray like a devotee in a temple to appease the guardian deity. But did it ever happen that the soldier or the worker or the devotee appeared on the scene before the theory had been either sensed or duly formulated? The fact of the matter is that since theory and practice are essential to one another and appear and disappear together, it follows that a soldier, as such, no more fights than a theory, as such, does.

What the young folk were in deep earnestness asked to remember was that it was only the theory that the Search formulated. Its main function did not extend any further. It was for the state to cover the rest. It was for it to raise the structure of government and administer the interests of the people. And if by any chance the state went the right way about building up that structure, it would have the goodwill and wholehearted support of the communities and the Search.

And here, before the session closed, the function of the Search as a specialized body was, once again, formulated, especially in its relation to that of the state and other specialized bodies in the society of man.

The Search was out, pre-eminently, to discover the Truth. That forms its chief objective and no other movement or institution is so directly interested in the Truth as the Search. So long as the Truth had not been found, the origin of the three organizations in history which have been formulated by the Search and the ethics of mutual abstention which followed from them, could not adequately be traced. This meant that a fresh view of Reality — which alone can explain the origin of history and indicate the future stages of the universe — would be formulated by the Search. And even after that formulation the Search would have to work out its own constitution and make provision for the regulation of the conduct of its members. In no part of all this very serious work would it function except as a detached body apart from the state and society. In fact, its main contribution to that society would lie wholly in exploring the future prospects of the human species and formulating a structure of society in which warfare could have no place.

To assess its claim to existence at the moment it need only be pointed out that the Search has provided the state with a review of history; a review which should convince the state that there is no longer any room for warfare. The state can now easily make up its mind to replace the method of warfare by the method of mutual abstention if it is so inclined.

But the Search does not claim the right of coercing the state in any form; not to speak of making it accept the method of mutual abstention if it does not spontaneously find its way to accepting it. And the main ground for that decision is that the issue when, exactly, an ethical principle should come into operation is not an issue of compulsion or persuasion. Indeed, how, exactly, and when the state should replace warfare by mutual abstention is nothing short of an issue for cosmic decision. Since the universe made provision for warfare for the whole period of history up to the present there is certainly nothing which should be called diabolic in the nature of warfare. Even though the Search has found that the basis on which warfare has stood is illusory, it has no right to conclude that warfare should on that account at once drop out of existence or ought never to have found a place in the cosmic scheme. All that the Search can legitimately hold is that the lifespan of warfare is by no means unlimited. But when exactly that span will finally come to an end — and how — is a cosmic issue and beyond the competence of the Search to explore. The Search is fully convinced that if illusion could rule the universe ever since it passed into the stage of what we call history it could well continue ruling it still. In other words, if both the rational and the irrational had a chance of functioning in the universe so far, there must have been some goodness in them both, whatever it might be. The universe will have to be shared from now between three distinct agencies: the rational, the irrational and the Truth. And that means necessarily a gradual and steady disappearance of the rule of illusion as time moves on.

We are indeed in a very curious position in the universe today — there are three masters for us to serve: Truth, Reason and Unreason. The Search has chosen the Truth and the state, though in a dubious way, is still hanging on to what it calls reason and unreason.

It was time now to disperse the Meeting and the philosopher had to give a short address to close the session. Summoning all the earnestness and force at his command he made his final comment on history, emphasizing once more that peace would never come to the human home if we still persisted in achieving it by warfare, whether violent or non-violent. It was inconceivable that the mystic, the humanist and the dualist could join hands and live together in peace if they were reduced to dealing with the incompatibilities between their main objectives by violent or non-violent warfare. The incompatibilities would remain, however endless the warfare: by this long-trodden route it would be impossible for them ever to arrive at their goal or to achieve peace.

And what enormous proportions this Armageddon would gradually reach from eon to eon one can only dimly visualize in the light of the panorama in which it must be set as it moves on. The strictly human phase of it which we know so well will soon be reduced to a mere speck or detail by contrast with the rest: and then the non-human range of that Armageddon will begin and keep steadily broadening till its vastness coincides with the bounds which space and time have set for our universe. It is a cruel Utopian who calmly sits down to calculate the time it will take the protons or the bacteria to finish their rounds of bitter conflict with all the other species on this earth. Even if the pace of evolution is forced by the super atoms yet to be known, it is a question whether even the sun, the giver of life, will choose to continue giving out heat for such a noble purpose as letting conflict run to the bitter end. It is lunacy to expect that peace will come in the end if the method of warfare is pushed to its logical limit.

Perhaps this is the only lunacy we have been subject to, so far!

But if, perchance, warfare is put away for good by the Cosmic — as we put away the steps as we walk — and mutual abstention firmly and unmistakably takes its place, there is no reason why the prospects of real peace and harmony should not arise at once: and then even the planets in the sky which have hitherto shed light on the field of warfare may suddenly lose their primeval sheen. Indeed there cannot but be an immediate change in the whole outlook of our globe, whose peak will be reached when all the creatures in its vast environment come to shed their age-long illusions and pride — their respect for the law of causation and for chance. And after that it will be a question of time when the diabolic distinction which the historian has drawn between the man and the ape or the ape and the reptile or the reptile and the vegetable fungus will dissolve as a dream.

And why indeed should not the ape and the reptile abstain if man or any other creature inevitably does? Did man — or even the gods — follow any law other than that of causation; or failing that, just pure chance? And who taught them? And what did the ape and the reptile follow if not exactly the same as they did? And who taught the ape and the reptile? It seemed as if the Voice was speaking again through the mouth of the philosopher.

The whole assembly at this stage acclaimed the philosopher and moved their support of the view that the state should not postpone any longer the dawn of the true era of Peace.

And the young descendants of the ruling clique took an oath that they would desert the state if it did not follow the Search altogether.

14

It is strange that there should be no record left in any way of what actually happened to the Search or to the state after the final Meeting of this session. Only three things are known: the Search did definitely reach its destination; the Truth was discovered; and the Mystic was proved to be absolutely in the right. But neither the states old or new nor the communities who belonged to them were taken into the confidence of the Search about the Truth which definitely came into its possession. For all practical purposes the Search completely disappeared, as all deeply esoteric bodies in tradition always did. Only unlike any esoteric body of tradition the Search left behind a reason for not passing on the Truth to the communities or to the states: the reason as formulated was that Truth is earned as a matter of course by all — in whatever station they might be — provided there is a real sense of need for it. In the opinion of the Search the need for Truth and its appearance necessarily come together. In no other way than by need can one get at the Truth. If, indeed, the need has not arisen it will be perfectly futile on the part of any individual or any group to make a demand for it as a matter of right; or to seek to find it by thought or action as dictated by the various traditional codes. When exactly the need will arise — and how — is not altogether a matter of chance, or *lila,* as the Hindus say, there is no such thing in the universe. There is almost a command which rigidly conditions the arrival of the need and that command is that human mind must come out of the illusion which history so far has cast on all existence. And this condition can be fulfilled now that the true nature of history is known and warfare can be replaced by the ethics of mutual abstention. If an individual or a group, whatever its proportions, comes to accept the analysis of history which the Search has developed the appearance of the need in them for the Truth will be but a question of time. But acceptance cannot be forced on anybody any more than the Truth can be seen as a matter of right or even of ascetic practice. Whatever, therefore, may be the significance of the fact that the Search conveyed the account of history and proved its truth — even by action and at enormous sacrifice — it did not entitle the Search to dogmatize about the future of the states or about their need. It is for the universe to decide when exactly the states will be relieved of their panoply of might.

There is a saying in the world today that a trail of light was left behind as the Search chose to disappear like an esoteric body. That light appears in different forms to different people who see it. To some it is like the tropical dawn which breaks on the stillness of a green earth; to others it is like the aurora borealis which scatters the Northern gloom. To those who see it at all times of the day or night it is like the eternal spring which the pilgrims expected would melt the snow into rivers bounding to the expectant plains. To one and all who see it, it is the third answer in the Dream as it began with the towering wave retreating from the dam.